On Location 1

Reading and Writing for Success in the Content Areas

Thomas Bye

McGraw-Hill

On Location 1

Published by McGraw-Hill ESL/ELT, a business unit of The McGraw-Hill Companies, Inc., 1221 Avenue of the Americas, New York, NY 10020. Copyright © 2005 by the McGraw-Hill Companies, Inc. All rights reserved. No part of this publication may be reproduced or distributed in any form or by any means, or stored in a database or retrieval system, without the prior written consent of The McGraw-Hill Companies, Inc., including, but not limited to, in any network or other electronic storage or transmission, or broadcast for distance learning.

ISBN 13: 978-0-07-288669-6
ISBN 10: 0-07-288669-2
3 4 5 6 7 8 9 10 QPD/QPD 11 10 09 08 07 06

ISBN 13: 978-0-07-111886-6 (International Student Edition)
ISBN 10: 0-07-111886-1 (International Student Edition)
1 2 3 4 5 6 7 8 9 10 QPD/QPD 11 10 09 08 07 06 05

Editorial director: Tina B. Carver
Executive editor: Erik Gundersen
Senior developmental editor: Mari Vargo
Developmental editors: Fredrik Liljeblad, Stephen Handorf
Production manager: Juanita Thompson
Cover designer: Wee Design Group
Interior designer: Wee Design Group
Artists: Burgundy Beam, Randy Chewning, Greg Harris, Albert Lorenz, Judy Love, Anni Matsick, George Ulrich
Photo researchers: David Averbach, Tobi Zausner
Skills indexer: Susannah MacKay

International Edition ISBN 0-07-111886-1
Copyright © 2005. Exclusive rights by The McGraw-Hill Companies, Inc., for manufacture and export. This book cannot be re-exported from the country to which it is sold by McGraw-Hill. The International Edition is not available in North America.

www.esl-elt.mcgraw-hill.com

The *McGraw-Hill* Companies

Acknowledgments

The authors and publisher would like to thank the following individuals who reviewed the *On Location* program at various stages of development and whose comments, reviews, and assistance were instrumental in helping us shape the project.

Carolyn Bohlman
Main East High School
Chicago, IL

Claire Bonskowski
Fairfax Public Schools
Fairfax, VA

Karen Caddoo
Sheridan Public Schools
Sheridan, CO

Florence Decker
El Paso MS/HS
Franklin, TX

Trudy Freer-Alvarez
Houston Independent School District
Houston, TX

Maryann Lyons
Francisco Middle School
San Francisco, CA

Susan Nordberg
Miami, FL

Jeanette Roy
Miami-Dade County Public Schools
Miami, FL

Steve Sloan
James Monroe High School
North Hills, CA

Leslie Eloise Somers
Miami-Dade County Public Schools
Miami, FL

Marie Stuart
San Gabriel Unified School District
San Gabriel, CA

Susan J. Watson
Horace Mann Middle School
San Francisco, CA

About the Author

Thomas Bye is an educator and consultant in second language learning and teaching. He was a high school teacher and has served as coordinator of bilingual education as well as director of curriculum and strategic planning for a large school district. He has written other programs for English Learners. He is an adjunct faculty member at St. Mary's College. He holds a Ph.D. in linguistics from UCLA.

Dedication

On Location is dedicated to my family, David Bohne and Chipper.

Scope and Sequence

Unit	Readings	Genres/ Writing Tasks	Reading Strategies	Word Work/ Spelling and Phonics
1 All about Me! page 2	Frame and name collages from the Internet	Personal information: "Me" collages	Using pictures to understand written information	Adjectives that describe people Pronouncing words with the letter *i*
2 Signs page 20	Selections from the book *Signs*	Environmental print: signs and symbols	Using pictures and images to understand environmental print	Root words Pronouncing words with the letter *a*
3 My Web Page page 38	Personal Web pages on the Internet	Personal Web pages Sentences	Using pictures to predict	Compound words Pronouncing words with the pattern *o* + consonant + *e*
4 Where Are We? page 56	Selections from *Looking at Maps and Globes*	Maps and mapping	Using pictures and visuals to understand written information	Antonyms Spelling the /s/ sound as in *miss* and *city*
5 Mean and Lazy page 74	Selections from *The Meanest: Amazing Facts about Mean Animals* and *The Laziest: Amazing Facts about Lazy Animals*	Informational writing: field guide	Finding details	Word groups: size, length, and weight Pronouncing words with the letter *a*

Grammar	Organization	Style	Writing Conventions	Content Area Connections	Links to Literature
The verb *be*	Organizing information in categories	Expressing meaning with visual images	Capitalization with the names of people	Art Math	Name poem
Imperatives	Organizing information in categories	Expressing meaning with visual images	Capitalization with the names of towns and cities	Civics	Poem "NO" by Shel Silverstein
Complete sentences	Organizing information in categories	Expressing meaning with visual images	End-of-sentence punctuation	Computers Graphing (Column Charts)	Autobiography poem
Plural nouns	Using elements of maps	Using features and conventions of maps	Capitalization with place names on maps and globes	Geography (location, measurement terms, landforms)	Poem "Number Four" by Charlotte Pomerantz
Subject-verb agreement	Using elements of field guides	Using precise adjectives	Using colons to introduce information	Animal life Geography Measurement: size and weight	Alphabet poem

Scope and Sequence

Unit	Readings	Genres/ Writing Tasks	Reading Strategies	Word Work/ Spelling and Phonics
6 You Can Cook! page 92	Recipes from the *Everything® Kids' Cookbook*	How-to instructions: recipes	Visualizing	Compound words Idioms Spelling the /k/ sound as in *king* and *cat*
7 Top Five page 110	Feature articles from *Time for Kids*	Surveys	Comparing Note taking	Word families: related nouns and verbs Words with digraphs
8 Memories page 128	Selections from "My First Sports Memory," from *Sports Illustrated for Kids*	Personal memories	Questioning the author	Synonyms Pronouncing words with silent consonants
9 Tall, Taller, Tallest page 146	Selections from *Hottest, Coldest, Highest, Deepest*	Short reports: our world	Using visuals to understand written information	Ordinal numbers Reading words with *i* + consonant + *e*
10 What Do You Think? page 164	Pro and con opinion columns from *Sports Illustrated for Kids*	Opinion columns	Evaluating ideas	Word families: related nouns and adjectives Spelling the sound /ī/ as in *my* and *high*

Grammar	Organization	Style	Writing Conventions	Content Area Connections	Links to Literature
Prepositions of location	Using elements of how-to instructions; time order	Using snappy names and titles	Numbering: time order	Measurement: amounts Nutrition Home Economics	Recipe poem
Present tense questions	Structuring of a report of information	Writing introductions that grab the reader's attention	Numbering: order of importance	Fractions, decimals, percent Graphing (pie charts)	List poem
Simple past tense	Using elements of personal narrative	Using descriptive adjectives	Capitalization of pronouns	Athletics	Memory poem
Comparatives and superlatives	Organizing an informational paragraph	Combining sentences	Exclamation points	Geography (location, measurement terms, landforms) Graphing (pictographs)	Diamante poem
Making comparisons: *as…as, more…than*	Using elements of opinion columns	Using quoted words in writing	Punctuation with quotation marks	Civics	Poem "Point of View" by Shel Silverstein

To the Student

Welcome to *On Location*! This book is written just for you. *On Location* will help you learn English while you explore the world.

You will read and write about our world—about killer snakes and lizards that are over nine feet long!

You will read and write about interesting people—other students just like you and sports stars with stories to tell.

Should boys play on girls' sports teams? You will find out what other students think and express your own ideas in writing.

You will read works by famous poets and poems by students. Then you'll write your own poems.

You will learn new words and skills that will help you in your other classes, such as math, science, social studies, and geography.

Best of all, you will get to work with others—talking, thinking, and making things as you learn English together.

This is going to be a great year. Enjoy the learning process!

Tom Bye

To the Teacher

Welcome to *On Location*—a three-level reading and writing program that provides an enrichment approach to language and literacy development. Specially designed for middle and high school students at beginning to intermediate levels, *On Location* provides a gradual onramp to academic English, allowing English learners the time they need to develop powerful academic reading, writing, and communications skills.

The *On Location* program offers a research-based approach that honors the findings of the National Reading Panel regarding the direct teaching of reading skills combined with the promotion of instructional practices that develop language and literacy through a focus on comprehension. *On Location* also supports the principles of the Cognitive Academic Language Learning Approach (CALLA), teaching learning strategies that help students succeed across the curriculum.

The program recognizes that learning to read and write is developmental, requiring the acquisition of listening and speaking skills and high levels of student engagement. *On Location* provides students with the direct skills instruction they need to master state and local standards within the context of meaningful communication.

On Location promotes the reading-writing connection through a focus on key academic genres—the kinds of writing students encounter in content-area classes and on high-stakes tests. Students read selections that describe, tell a story, analyze, explain, justify a position, and persuade. And they explore the organizational and stylistic features of each genre as they produce their own writing.

PROVIDING AN ON-RAMP TO ACADEMIC LANGUAGE

Student Books

On Location is organized into three levels. Book 1 enables students to meet beginning-level standards for reading, writing, and oral language. Reading selections are fewer than 100 words in length, building basic fluency and comprehension skills. By the end of Book 1, students are able to read simple paragraphs and write well-formed, connected sentences.

Book 2 enables students to meet early intermediate standards. Reading selections are under 300 words in length, providing access to authentic text materials. By the end of Book 2, students are able to read simple multi-paragraph selections and write related paragraphs.

Book 3 enables students to meet intermediate-level standards. Reading selections are less than 800 words in length, providing an onramp to academic text. By the end of Book 3, students are able to produce simple essays—writing that informs, explains, analyzes, and persuades.

The *On Location* books are organized into ten engaging units, each focusing on a particular nonfiction reading and writing genre. Every reading is authentic—giving students opportunities to read a variety of real-world text selections. Because the reading selections come from sources such as *Junior Scholastic* and *Time for Kids*—as well as the Internet—they are always engaging and help students connect to the world around them.

In each unit, students have the opportunity to produce the type of writing that the unit's reading selection exemplifies. Incorporating a "backwards build-up" model, this is how a unit works—

- Students begin by connecting the topic of the unit's reading selections to their own lives and by developing key vocabulary they will need to read with understanding.
- Students tackle a word analysis skill and explore a grammatical structure they will encounter in each reading.

- As students read the selections that model the genre, they work at building fluency and develop reading strategies that help them become active readers.
- After reading, students explore the organization patterns and stylistic features of the selections.
- Students then produce their own writing as they move through the stages of the writing process that culminates with an oral presentation to classmates.

Along the way, students engage in structured listening and speaking activities that promote thinking and discussion, develop understanding, and build motivation. They explore sound/spelling relationships of words and learn common written conventions.

Each unit opens doors to academic content. Students explore topics in science, social studies, and geography and learn essential academic vocabulary and skills to help them tackle grade-level content across the curriculum. Students also read and respond to a literature selection in each unit that relates to the content of the readings in that unit.

On Location is designed for use in a variety of classroom settings.

SCENARIOS	TIME FRAME	STRATEGIES FOR USE
1: **On Location** serves as the primary instructional program.	12–18 hours/unit	Complete all Student Book and Practice Book activities. Implement all suggestions in the Teacher's Edition. Use all components of the On Location assessment system.
2: **On Location** supplements an adopted basal program, providing students with intensive reading/writing instruction.	8–12 hours/unit	Complete sections B through H in the Student Book. Complete selected Practice Book activities. Use Teacher's Edition suggestions as needed.
3: Selected units from **On Location** supplement an adopted basal program, providing opportunities to read and write non-fiction.	5–8 hours/unit	Complete sections B, C, F, G, and H in the Student Book. Use Teacher's Edition suggestions as needed.

Practice Books

Each level of On Location includes a corresponding **Practice Book**. The Practice Book provides students with the opportunity to master the reading skills, vocabulary, and grammar introduced in the Student Book while allowing them to evaluate their own writing and practice test-taking skills. Activities allow students to further explore unit topics, respond to literature selections, and discover how much they learned by completing the activities and writing tasks in the Student Books.

Audio Program

An **audio program** also accompanies each level of On Location. The audio program includes activities that develop social and academic listening skills in addition to recordings of all of the reading selections.

Phonics Book

On Location Phonics, which can be used as an introduction to *On Location* or in parallel fashion with Book 1, provides systematic, explicit instruction that helps students who are new to English hear the sound patterns of their new language and use knowledge of sound-letter relationships to read and write high-frequency words and phrases that they hear and see around them. Incorporating a "fast-track" approach, this optional component enables newcomers to learn both language and content from day one. Teaching notes at the bottom of each student page make *On Location Phonics* a self-contained program.

PROMOTING STAFF DEVELOPMENT

Wrap-Around Teacher's Editions

A wrap-around **Teacher's Edition** provides step by step guidance through every lesson, helping the teacher use best teaching practices to—

- introduce new vocabulary and important concepts through use of context
- use a three-stage process to develop active readers that involves reading aloud ("my turn"), having students share the reading task ("our turn"), and independent reading ("your turn")
- guide students through the stages of the writing process.

Teacher Training and Staff Development Video

The *On Location* program includes a powerful staff development video to support implementation of the program. The video provides strategies for teaching reading and writing from a language arts perspective—focusing on best practices such as pre-teaching vocabulary, use of read aloud/think aloud techniques, interactive reading, modeled writing, interactive writing, use of rubrics, and cooperative learning. The training video provides strategies for reading and writing in the content areas and demonstrates how *On Location* can be used effectively.

ENSURING ADEQUATE YEARLY PROGRESS

Assessment System

The *On Location* **Assessment System** includes a placement test, end-of-unit assessments, and end-of-level tests. Task-specific rubrics (or "ChecBrics") help students plan, revise, and evaluate their work.

Teachers can be sure that with its emphasis on academic reading and writing, *On Location* will help their school meet Adequate Yearly Progress (AYP) targets. The *On Location* assessment system supports district accountability efforts by providing tools that enable teachers to evaluate mastery of English language development/English language arts standards.

Welcome to On Location

On Location is a three-level supplementary series that teaches middle-school and high-school English learners to read and write non-fiction. Its gradual on-ramp approach gives learners the time and support they need to develop powerful academic reading, writing, and communication skills.

Tuning In activities provide **engaging listening passages** which introduce students to the topic of each unit.

Useful vocabulary is introduced throughout each unit. Students learn new words that will help them understand reading passages, discuss their ideas, and complete their own writing.

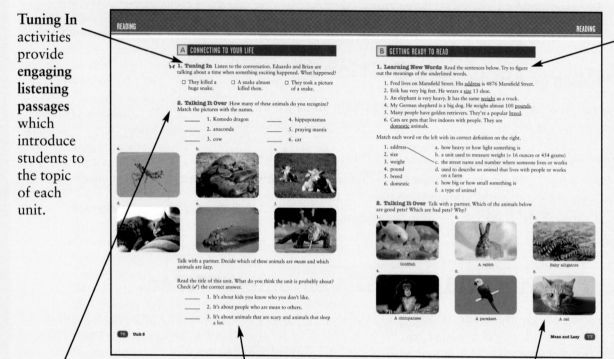

Students have multiple **opportunities to discuss ideas** with partners and in groups. **Talking It Over** provides context for the upcoming reading and writing activities. It **makes connections to students' experiences, challenges them to think, and promotes classroom discussion.**

The **predictable organization** of each unit combined with the **variety of genres and topics** provides a **comfortable yet motivating experience** for students.

Vibrant and compelling art and photos bring units to life, illustrating ideas and vocabulary words related to the unit's topic and genre.

Let's Read contains information about the upcoming reading selection and provides a question or a task that **helps students focus their reading.**

Before You Read activates background knowledge and connects students to the reading topic.

In **Unlocking Meaning**, three activities help students **understand what they are reading and encourage them to reread.** First, students identify the main idea, argument, or proposition. Second, they find details, reasons, or examples. And finally, they think more deeply about the reading.

Reading passages are accompanied by **relevant and practical reading strategies** that help students **develop a personal set of reading comprehension skills.**

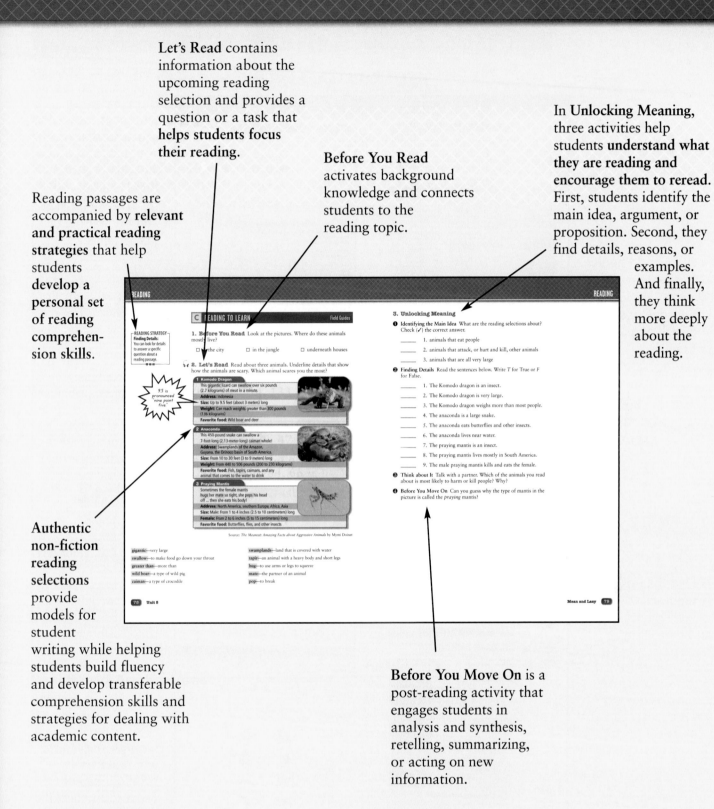

Authentic non-fiction reading selections provide models for student writing while helping students build fluency and develop transferable comprehension skills and strategies for dealing with academic content.

Before You Move On is a post-reading activity that engages students in analysis and synthesis, retelling, summarizing, or acting on new information.

Grammar lessons provide instruction and practice around a **grammar point that is relevant to the reading passages and the writing task** in each unit.

Spelling and Phonics activities help students develop knowledge of **sound** and **spelling patterns** in English.

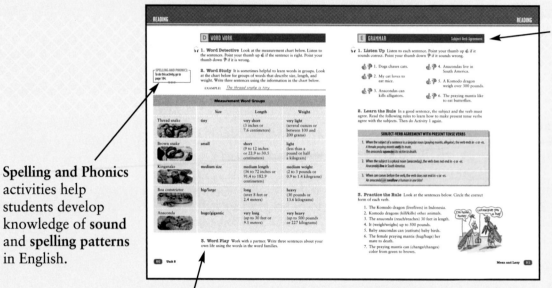

Activities in the *Word Work* section develop word-analysis skills that help students figure out the meaning of vocabulary in the content areas.

Making Content Connections activities provide opportunities for students to complete tasks that relate to content areas, such as geography, science, and math.

A recording of every reading selection is included in the audio program.

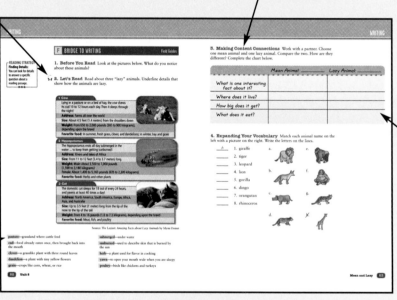

Graphic organizers and other tools promote **higher order thinking skills**, such as comparing, synthesizing, and inferencing.

New words are **glossed** below reading selections and are included in the glossary at the back of the book.

The sequence of activities in the *Writing Clinic* and the *Writer's Workshop* provides students with step-by-step procedures for producing a well-formed piece of academic writing. Students can use these procedures to complete writing assignments in their content area classes.

In **Focus on Organization** and **Focus on Style** activities, students **analyze the selection they have just read.**

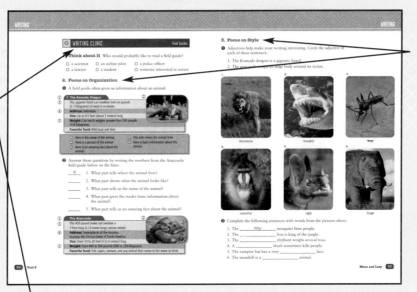

In **Getting It Out** activities, students learn new strategies and work with lists, images, and graphic organizers to plan and develop their own writing.

After students have decided on their topics, they use a graphic organizer, a set of questions, or a specific set of instructions to guide them in their information gathering.

Students work gradually toward completing their writing assignments. First, they spend time choosing the topic they'd like to write about.

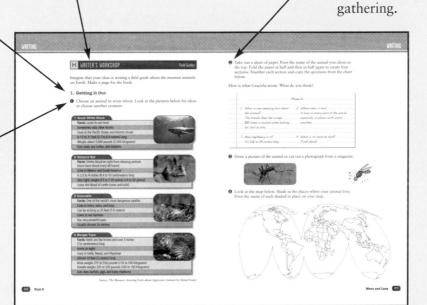

In Getting It Down, students turn their brainstorming and planning work into an outline and then a first-draft. Models are provided to demonstrate to students exactly what they are expected to do.

Getting It Right provides students with a combined checklist and rubric ("ChecBric") that helps them evaluate and revise their writing. The ChecBric, which is specific to each writing task, focuses on the skills that students have learned in the unit and provides a basis for evaluating level of performance on the task.

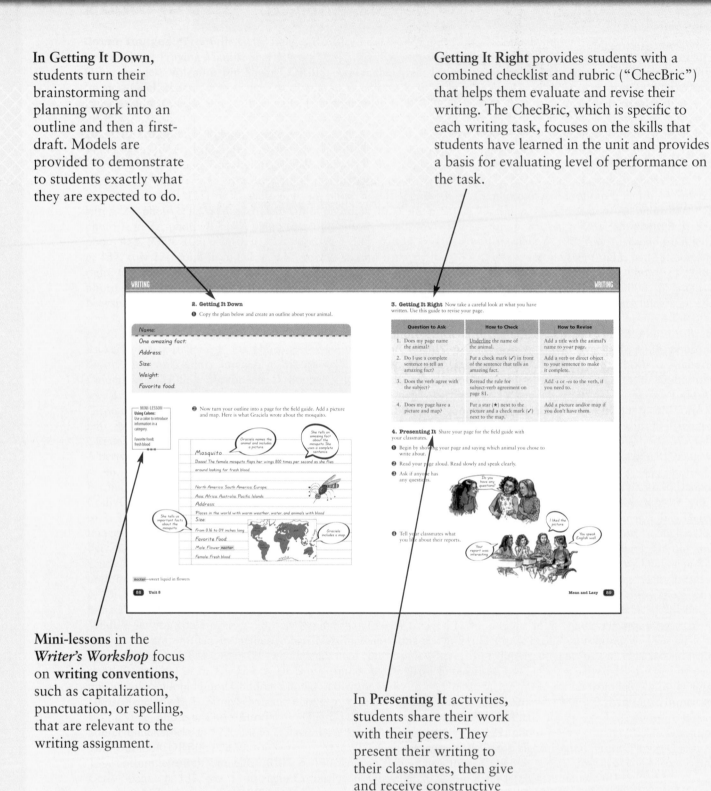

Mini-lessons in the *Writer's Workshop* focus on **writing conventions,** such as capitalization, punctuation, or spelling, that are relevant to the writing assignment.

In **Presenting It** activities, students share their work with their peers. They present their writing to their classmates, then give and receive constructive feedback.

On Assignment activities provide fun exercises related to unit topics. Students learn more about each topic and interact with their classmates while they participate in class art shows, make posters, and conduct interviews.

In **Link to Literature** activities, students read poems or fiction selections and participate in guided discussions.

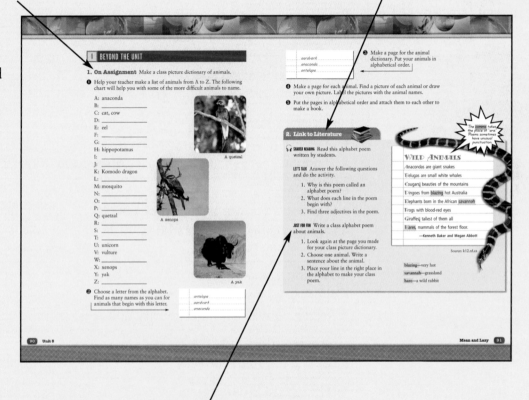

After reading and discussing a selection, students do something **Just for Fun**, such as adding lines to a poem or writing their own poems.

All about Me!

Read...

- "Me" collages. Learn about what other students are like.

Link to Literature

- Name poems written by students.

Objectives:

Reading:
- Understanding words and phrases
- Strategy: Connecting visuals with text
- Literature: Reading poetry

Writing:
- Personal information: Making a "me" collage
- Organizing information into categories
- Choosing images and words to describe yourself

Vocabulary:
- Learning adjectives that describe people
- Learning names of things students like (foods, school subjects, sports)

Listening/Speaking:
- Finding out more about others
- Talking about things that you like and are good at

Grammar:
- Using the verb *be* correctly

Spelling and Phonics:
- Pronouncing words with the letter *i*

Collage by Connie, Grade 9

BEFORE YOU BEGIN

Talk with your classmates.

1. Look at the collage. What do you see?
   ☐ photographs   ☐ drawings   ☐ words
2. Read the caption. Who made the collage?
3. Help your teacher make a list of the things you see in the collage.

A CONNECTING TO YOUR LIFE

1. Tuning In Listen to a boy talk about what he likes. Point your thumb up 👍 if you like the same thing. Point your thumb down 👎 if you do not.

2. Talking It Over Look at the pictures and descriptions below. Walk around your classroom and find one person for each description. Write the person's name on the line.

Find someone who...

...likes to read.

...is good at sports.

...likes pizza.

1. _____

2. _____

3. _____

...speaks three languages.

...likes math.

...plays basketball.

4. _____

5. _____

6. _____

...likes to watch TV.

...is a nice person.

...likes music.

7. _____

8. _____

9. _____

Read the title of this unit. What do you think the unit is probably about? Check (✔) the correct answer.

_____ 1. It's all about sports.

_____ 2. It's all about animals.

_____ 3. It's all about you.

B **GETTING READY TO READ**

1. Learning New Words Read the sentences below. Try to figure out the meanings of the underlined words.

    1. I speak *five* languages. I am <u>special</u>!

    2. I like being with other kids. I have a lot of <u>friends</u>!

    3. I like <u>sports</u>. I like baseball, basketball, and football.

    4. A lot of people like me. I am <u>popular</u>.

    5. I always get an A+ in every class. I am the <u>best</u> student in school.

    6. My friend Tran is a very nice person. He is <u>loveable</u>.

Match each word on the left with the correct definition on the right.

1. special	a. games people or teams play against each other
2. friend	b. having a lot of friends
3. sports	c. different from most other people and things
4. popular	d. easy for other people to love
5. best	e. someone you like and who likes you
6. loveable (*also spelled* lovable)	f. better than anyone or anything else

2. Talking It Over Talk with a partner. Share three or four things that make you special.

I speak two languages.

I play the violin.

I'm a really good soccer player.

C   READING TO LEARN   "Me" Collages

READING STRATEGY
Using Pictures:
When you see pictures and words together, the pictures can help you understand the meaning of the words.

1. Before You Read Write down a word that says something about *you*. Share what you wrote with a partner. Word: _____

2. Let's Read Look at Juan's "me collage." Read the words and sentences that make the frame.

The frame is the part that goes around the picture.

hip-hop—a type of music that lots of kids like

Wow!—what you say when something surprises you

3. Unlocking Meaning

❶ **Identifying the Main Idea** Who are the words in the collage about? Check (✔) the correct answer.

_____ 1. the boy in the picture

_____ 2. the boy's best friend

_____ 3. the boy's family

❷ **Finding Details** Look at the collage again. Some of the words have letters next to them. Match the words to the sentences below. Write the letters on the lines.

___*b*___ 1. The boy in the picture is named Juan.

_____ 2. Juan is a happy person. He smiles a lot.

_____ 3. Juan always works hard.

_____ 4. Juan has many friends.

_____ 5. Juan likes football and basketball.

_____ 6. Juan is one of a kind.

_____ 7. Juan likes himself.

❸ **Think about It** List three things you are good at. Choose from the activities below, or think of different ones. Share your list with a partner.

1. _____   2. _____   3. _____

1.

math

2.

baseball

3.

cooking

4.

dancing

5.

drawing

6.

basketball

❹ **Before You Move On** Make a sign for your desk with a frame. Write words about you on the frame. Then tape the sign to your desk.

D WORD WORK

Matt

1. Word Detective Listen to Juan and Lori talk about their friends. Point your thumb up 👍 if you would like the person as a friend. Point your thumb down 👎 if you would not.

1. Maria is funny.
2. Stefan is quiet.
3. Zaida is friendly.
4. Matt is athletic.
5. Wen-Ying is nice.
6. Sau-Lim is shy.

2. Word Study Adjectives are words that describe nouns. They can sometimes be positive 😊 or negative 😞.

😊	😞
Maria is a **nice** girl.	Stefan is a **lazy** kid.
Lori is always **polite**.	Zaida is sometimes **rude**.

3. Word Play Work with a partner. Decide if each of the following adjectives is positive 😊 or negative 😞. Color in your choices. Then write two sentences with positive adjectives and two sentences with negative adjectives. You can use your dictionary.

| smart | 😊 😞 | lazy | 😊 😞 | friendly | 😊 😞 | mean | 😊 😞 |
| beautiful | 😊 😞 | popular | 😊 😞 | loud | 😊 😞 | stupid | 😊 😞 |

Positive:
1. _____
2. _____

Negative:
1. _____
2. _____

┌─ SPELLING AND PHONICS: ─┐
To do this activity, go to
page 182.
■ ■ ■

E | GRAMMAR The Verb *Be*

1. Listen Up Listen to each sentence. Point your thumb up 👍 if it sounds correct. Point your thumb down 👎 if it sounds wrong.

👍 👎 1. I am a student.

👍 👎 2. You is a very nice person.

👍 👎 3. Juan and Maria is in the ninth grade.

👍 👎 4. They are good friends.

👍 👎 5. We are both in the ninth grade.

👍 👎 6. Juan and Maria is good students.

2. Learn the Rule Now read the following rules for the verb *be*, then repeat Activity 1.

THE VERB *BE*		
1. The verb *be* must agree with the subject of the sentence. Sometimes the subject is a noun (*Juan*, *bicycle*), and sometimes it is a pronoun (*he*, *it*).		
*I **am** a student.*	*You **are** a student.*	*Juan **is** a student. He **is** in ninth grade.*
2. When you talk, you usually use the subject pronoun + the short form of the verb *be*. This is called a contraction.		
I'm a student.	*You're a student.* (1 person)	*He's a student.*
We're students.	*You're students.* (2+ people)	*They're students.*

3. Practice the Rule Work with a partner. Complete each sentence below with the correct full form of the verb *be*. Then say each sentence aloud, using the short form when it is possible.

1. I _____ in the ninth grade.
2. Tran _____ from Vietnam.
3. Juan and Maria _____ friends.
4. They _____ the same age.
5. You _____ a very nice person.
6. She _____ from Mexico.
7. We _____ both ninth graders.
8. Ms. Lee said, "You _____ all good students."

F BRIDGE TO WRITING   "Me" Collages

READING STRATEGY
Using Pictures:
When you see pictures
and words together, the
pictures can help you
understand the
meaning of the words.

1. Before You Read Write down three things you love. Share your
list with a partner.

1. _____   2. _____   3. _____

2. Let's Read Look at Lori's collage. Make a list of the words that
you see. Circle the words that describe you too.

3. Making Content Connections On a separate piece of paper, draw a Venn diagram like this one. Compare yourself with Lori.

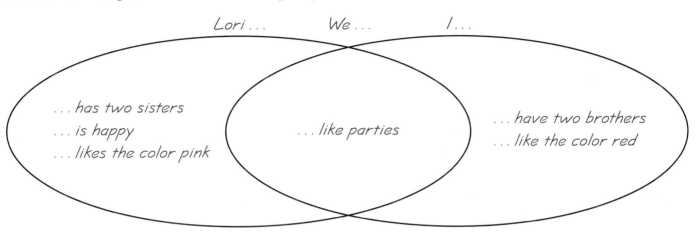

Lori . . .   *We . . .*   *I . . .*

. . . has two sisters
. . . is happy
. . . likes the color pink

. . . like parties

. . . have two brothers
. . . like the color red

4. Expanding Your Vocabulary What are some things that you like? Tell a partner.

I like fruit.

Foods

pizza   hot dog   fruit   ice cream cone   salad   tostada

School Subjects

English   math   science   PE   art   computers

Sports

football   baseball   volleyball   basketball   soccer   tennis

G WRITING CLINIC

"Me" Collages

1. Think about It Why would you make a "me" collage?

☐ to tell people who you are and what you like ☐ to make people laugh ☐ to tell a story about a friend

2. Focus on Organization

❶ Study the collage. Look at the lettered explanations below the collage for an explanation of each word or picture.

ⓐ This picture shows Lori.

ⓑ This picture shows Lori's family.

ⓒ This picture shows Lori with her friends.

ⓓ This word explains what Lori is like.

ⓔ This word explains what Lori likes.

ⓕ This word explains what Lori likes to do.

❷ Work with a partner. Look at Lori's collage again. Complete the chart below.

Words that explain what Lori is like	Words that explain what Lori likes	Words that explain what Lori likes to do
Loveable		

3. Focus on Style

"Me" collages often use photographs, drawings, and other images to illustrate what a person is like. Match each of the following images to the correct sentences below.

a.

b.

c.

d.

e.

f.

___c___ 1. I like to go to amusement parks.

_____ 2. I like purple.

_____ 3. I like to go to the beach.

_____ 4. I like baseball.

_____ 5. I like fast food hamburgers.

_____ 6. My family and I are from Mexico.

H WRITER'S WORKSHOP   "Me" Collages

Make a collage that tells your classmates what you are like and what you like to do.

1. Getting It Out

❶ Think about *what you are like, the things you like,* and *what you like to do.* Make an idea chart about yourself like the one below.

Words about me	What I like	What I like to do
funny	pizza	play sports
cute	funny movies	go to Eliza's
smart	books about	house
...	animals	listen to music
	...	...

❷ Collect images—words and pictures—that describe you and your life. Look at these examples for help.

1.

Pictures of you

2.

Pictures of your family
(and pets!)

3.

Pictures of you and your friends

4.

Pictures of things you like or
things you like to do

5.

Words and pictures
from magazines

6.

Words from food wrappers

2. Getting It Down

❶ Select the images you like best from those that you have collected.

❷ Place your images on a piece of paper. Do not paste them!
Here is Carlos's "me" collage. What do you think?

3. Getting It Right

❶ Take a careful look at your collage. Use this guide to help you revise your work.

Question to Ask	How to Check	How to Revise
1. Do I use both words and images?	Count the number of words and images in your collage.	Add more words or images.
2. Does my collage tell all about me?	Look again at your idea chart. Does your collage have words and pictures that say everything about you?	Add words or images that help tell more about you.
3. Is my collage nice to look at?	Make sure all parts of your collage go together.	Try moving words and images around to make them more attractive.

❷ Share your collage with two classmates. Talk about it. Ask them what they think.

❸ Finish your collage.

1.

Add words or pictures.

2.

Take away words or pictures.

3.

Put words or pictures in a different place.

4.

Glue each word or picture on a sheet of paper.

5.

Spray your work with sealant.

6.

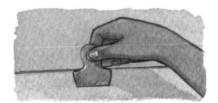

Attach a hook to the back.

4. Presenting It

❶ Share your collage with your classmates. Explain to the class three things your collage says about you.

❷ After each collage presentation by your classmates, say something nice about the work they have done.

1. On Assignment Display your collages. Have a class art show.

❶ Where will you display your collages? When? Talk it over as a class.

❷ Write your name and grade on the bottom half of an index card.

❸ Fold the index card in half. Make sure your name is on the inside. Paste the card to the bottom of your collage.

❹ Invite the art teacher at your school to be a judge of the Collage Art Show.

Dear Ms. Painter:

Please judge our Collage Art Show. It will take place on September 30. Thank you.

Sincerely, ELD I Class

❺ Invite other students or your family to come to the art show when you have it. Can friends and family guess who made each collage?

❻ Award prizes for "most colorful," "most descriptive," "funniest," "most beautiful," and "best" collages.

2. Link to Literature

SHARED READING Read these name poems written by students.

LET'S TALK Answer the following questions.

1. Why are these poems called "name poems"?
2. How is each poem different from the others?
3. Which poem do you like best? Why?

JUST FOR FUN Write your own name poem.

1. Begin each line with the letters, in order, of your first name.
2. Think of a word, phrase, or sentence for each letter that says something about you.
3. Write your poem on a separate piece of paper. Use color, if you wish. Share your name poem with your classmates.

My Name Poem

B is for Butterflies.
E is for Enjoy.
N is for Nature.

Brianna
Brat
Real
Innocent
Awesome
Naughty
Nice
Athletic

John
John is an athlete.
On Saturdays he likes to sleep in.
His favorite food is pizza.
Never call him Johnny.

Sources: diskovery.ltsc.org
saintmarysschools.com
abcteach.com

brat—a bad, difficult child

innocent—sweet or nice

awesome—really, really great

athletic—good at sports

sleep in—to get up later than you usually do

Signs

Read...

■ Selections from the book *Signs* by Susan Canizares and Pamela Chanko. Learn how signs tell us important messages in just a few words.

Link to Literature

■ "NO," a poem by Shel Silverstein.

Objectives:

Reading:
■ Understanding signs all around us
■ Understanding the jobs different types of signs have
■ Strategy: Using photos and visuals to understand meaning
■ Recognizing logos and symbols
■ Literature: Reading poetry

Writing:
■ Making signs
■ Organizing information into categories
■ Writing simple captions

Vocabulary:
■ Recognizing root words
■ Learning words on common signs in different places at school and in the community

Listening/Speaking:
■ Understanding simple conversations
■ Following commands
■ Listening to/giving feedback

Grammar:
■ Understanding imperatives

Spelling and Phonics:
■ Pronouncing words with the letter *a*

BEFORE YOU BEGIN

Talk with your classmates.

1. Look at the picture. What do you see?
2. What does the sign mean? What is the boy thinking about?
3. Help your teacher make a list of signs you see around you every day.

A CONNECTING TO YOUR LIFE

1. Tuning In Listen to the conversations. People are talking in different places. Where do you think the people are? Write your answers on the lines below.

1. *at a school*
2. _____
3. _____
4. _____
5. _____

2. Talking It Over Look at these signs. Which one does not belong with the others? How do you know? Talk with a partner. Then make a sign that you might see at Kennedy High School.

1.

2.

3.

4.

5.

6.

Read the title of this unit. What do you think the unit is probably about? Check (✓) the correct answer.

_____ 1. It's about learning the letters of the alphabet.

_____ 2. It's about learning what signs mean.

_____ 3. It's about learning school rules.

B GETTING READY TO READ

1. Learning New Words Read the sentences below. Try to figure out the meanings of the underlined words.

1. There is a large pile of snow and ice on the road. There was an <u>avalanche</u> yesterday!
2. Highway 80 is closed. We have to take a <u>detour</u> on another road.
3. Be careful! That sign says <u>danger</u>—we could get hurt.
4. A traffic guard helps kids cross the street. She stands at the school <u>crossing</u>.
5. Our school has a small lunch <u>area</u>. There is very little space during lunch.
6. People <u>deposit</u> their mail in a mailbox.

Match each word on the left with the correct definition on the right.

1. avalanche
2. detour
3. danger
4. crossing
5. area
6. deposit

a. to put something into something else
b. a part of a building, park, office, etc., for doing something
c. snow, ice, and rocks that fall off a mountain side
d. a harmful situation
e. a place where you can go from one side of the street to the other
f. a different way of going from one place to another

2. Talking It Over A sign is a board or poster in a public place with information on it. Work in small groups. Make a list of signs you see at school and in the community.

At School	In the Community
NO TALKING	TWO TACOS FOR 99¢

What does each sign mean? Tell your classmates about the signs on your list.

C **READING TO LEARN** **Signs**

1. Before You Read Look at the signs in these pictures. Which sign do you see most often in everyday life?

🎧 **2. Let's Read** You are going to read a book about signs. As you read, **use the pictures** to help you understand what each sign means.

Signs can tell you...

a.

...where you are.

b.

...where things go.

c.

...when to stop.

d.

...too much snow.

Source: *Signs* by Susan Canizares and Pamela Chanko

recycle—to use things again that people throw away

3. Unlocking Meaning

❶ Finding the Main Idea Look at the signs on page 24. What do they do? Check (✓) the correct answer.

_____ 1. They scare us.

_____ 2. They help us.

_____ 3. They make us laugh.

❷ Finding Details Match each of the following sign phrases to the correct picture below.

___e___ 1. STOP

_____ 2. AVALANCHE AREA

_____ 3. RAILROAD CROSSING

_____ 4. CROCODILE CROSSING

_____ 5. DANGER! THIN ICE

_____ 6. RECYCLE AREA

a.

b.

c.

d.

e.

f.

❸ Think about It What kinds of signs are helpful? Check (✓) the correct answers.

_____ 1. Signs that are easy to read.

_____ 2. Signs that are colorful.

_____ 3. Signs that are red.

_____ 4. Signs that use many pictures.

_____ 5. Signs that have special shapes.

_____ 6. Signs that use just a few words.

❹ Before You Move On Work with a partner. Make up a funny sign for your classroom.

D WORD WORK

1. Word Detective Sometimes you can figure out what a new word means by looking for a smaller word inside of it. Circle the smaller word inside each of the following underlined words.

1. NO SWIMMING.
2. NO FISHING.
3. NO EATING.
4. NO NAME-CALLING.
5. NO PUSHING.
6. NO CHEWING GUM.

2. Word Study Many verbs in English can be made into -*ing* nouns. Think of a sign at your school that uses an -*ing* noun. What is the verb?

VERB	NOUN
to **skateboard**	NO **SKATEBOARDING** ON CAMPUS
to **run**	NO **RUNNING** IN THE HALLS

3. Word Play Work with a partner. Make at least five signs using the verbs in the following table. Turn the verbs into -*ing* nouns.

EXAMPLE: NO SHOUTING INSIDE THE BUILDING

shout	sleep	fight
fight	wear	eat
talk	play	laugh

> **SPELLING AND PHONICS:**
> To do this activity, go to page 182.

E GRAMMAR   Commands

1. Listen Up Listen to these commands. Do what the person tells you to do.

1. Take out a piece of paper.
2. Pick up a pencil.
3. Write your name in the upper right-hand corner.
4. Draw a square on the paper.
5. Print "DO NOT TALK" on the paper.
6. Show your sign to a partner.

2. Learn the Rule Read the following rules to understand when to use commands. Then write two commands on the lines beneath the chart.

To be polite, add "Please..."

COMMANDS
When you want someone to do something, use a command.   ***Take out*** *a sheet of paper.*   ***Please take out*** *a sheet of paper.*
When you want someone not to do something, or to stop doing something, use "Do not..." or "Don't..."   ***Don't talk!***

Commands:

1. _____

2. _____

3. Practice the Rule Work in pairs. Complete items 11 and 12 with your own ideas. Tell your partner to do each of the following things.

EXAMPLES: Touch your head. Don't look at me.

1. to touch his or her head
2. to touch his or her shoulder
3. to shut his or her eyes
4. to open his or her eyes
5. to look at the ceiling
6. not to laugh at you
7. not to look at you
8. not to talk to you
9. not to bother you
10. not to sit next to you
11. to look at _____
12. not to _____

1. Before You Read Look around your classroom for a sign that begins with "NO" or "DON'T." What does the sign tell you?

 **2. Let's Read** Read the rest of the book on signs. Think of one more example of a "NO" sign.

Signs can also tell us...

e.

...not to fish.

f.

...not to walk.

g.

...not to swim.

h.

...not to talk

i.

...where to turn.

j.

...where to eat.

k.

...where to find a special treat!   Source: *Signs* by Susan Canizares and Pamela Chanko

diner—a restaurant with simple food and low prices   **special treat**—something good to eat

3. Making Content Connections Signs are important—especially at school. What can happen if you don't pay attention to signs? Talk it over with a partner. Then complete the chart below.

Signs can tell you...	Examples	If you don't pay attention to the sign...
...to be careful of something.	CAUTION! Wet floor	...you may slip and fall down
...to do something.		
...not to do something.		

4. Expanding Your Vocabulary Almost all places have signs to help you find things. For each place below, circle the sign that you would probably **not** see in that place.

1. A hospital: EMERGENCY   WAITING ROOM   (PRINCIPAL'S OFFICE)

2. A restaurant: PLEASE WAIT TO BE SEATED   PLEASE CLEAN UP AFTER YOUR DOG   DAILY SPECIALS

3. A mall: DIRECTORY   INFORMATION   NO HUNTING

4. An airport: NO RUNNING IN THE HALLS   CUSTOMS   BAGGAGE CLAIM AREA

5. A park: CASHIER   PICNIC AREA   DO NOT FEED THE DUCKS

6. A grocery store: PRODUCE   ARRIVALS   EXPRESS LINE

G **WRITING CLINIC** Signs

1. Think about It Where is one place you would probably not see a sign?

☐ at the market ☐ at school ☐ at the beach
☐ in an airplane ☐ in the sky ☐ along a road

2. Focus on Organization

❶ We see signs everywhere.

In towns and cities

Outdoors

Along streets and highways

In schools and libraries

"X-ing" is short for "crossing"

❷ Where would you probably find each of the following signs? Complete the chart below. Put each sign in the correct column.

Speed Limit 55	U-Turn OK	~~Sam's Market~~	School X-ing
Watch for Bears	Main Office	U.S. Post Office	No Running
Room 222	Elevation 5,000 Feet	Danger! Falling Rocks	Bijou Theatre

In the City	In the Outdoors	On Streets and Highways	At School
Sam's Market			

❸ Signs have many different jobs to do.

They tell you what to do...or what NOT to do.

They warn you of possible problems.

They help you know where you are.

They tell you where to go.

And, sometimes they make you want to eat, buy, or do something fun.

❹ Work with a partner. Create signs that do each of the following jobs:

- tell you what to do (or *not* to do)
- warn you

- help you
- make you want to do something

3. Focus On Style Signs often have logos. Logos are small designs that help you notice or remember a name or idea. Match each logo with the correct type of business below.

a.

b.

c.

d.

e.

f.

____d____ 1. a clothing store

_____ 2. a music and electronics store

_____ 3. a Web site

_____ 4. a nut supply company

_____ 5. a restaurant

_____ 6. a bank

H WRITER'S WORKSHOP   Signs

Your class is writing a "picture dictionary" of signs. Each page will be about signs that have the same job.

Job: Telling you what to do

Job: Telling you where you are

Job: Telling you about danger

Job: Making you want something

Each page should have three parts:

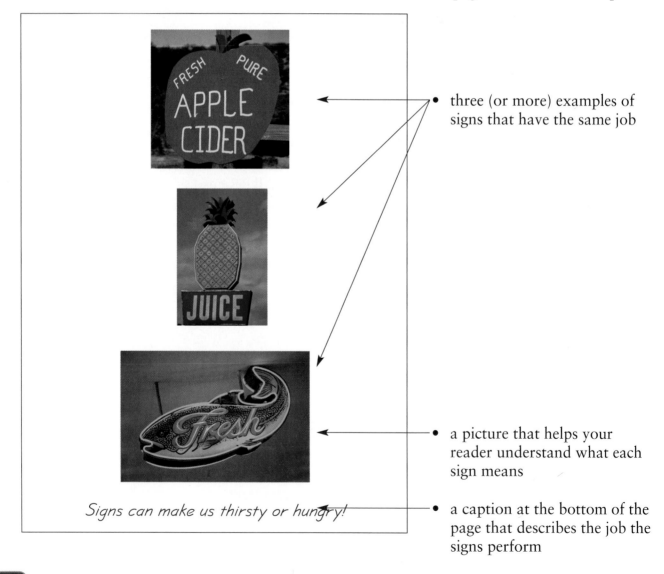

Signs can make us thirsty or hungry!

- three (or more) examples of signs that have the same job

- a picture that helps your reader understand what each sign means

- a caption at the bottom of the page that describes the job the signs perform

1. Getting It Out Take a field trip. Look for signs!

❶ First, develop a plan. Decide where you will look for signs.

☐ at school
☐ in your community
☐ on the road

❷ Before you begin looking for signs, you will need to get supplies for your field trip.

• notebook or clipboard
• pencil or pen
• colored markers or pencils

❸ Copy each sign you see. Draw the sign in your notebook *exactly* as you see it.

• Use the same words.
• Use the same shape.
• Use the same colors.

❹ After your field trip, sort your signs into groups by the job that they do.

Tell what...

California
US 99

Tell where...

Now entering
Los Angeles

Warn...

Proceed
with Caution

Make you want
something

Burger Queen
Next Offramp

2. Getting It Down

❶ Decide which signs you will put on each page of your picture dictionary.

❷ Draw pictures to show what the signs mean.

❸ Write a caption for each page. To practice, complete the captions below.

1.

Signs can

tell you where

you are .

2.

Signs can

_____

_____ .

3.

Signs can

_____

_____ .

4.

Signs can

_____

_____ .

❹ Here is a page from the book that Carlos made. What do you think?

The signs look real. The words, shapes, and colors are correct.

I like Carlos's picture of the freeway.

You see these signs along the freeway. They tell you were you are.

The caption explains what the signs do.

SIGNS CAN TELL YOU WHERE YOU ARE.

3. Getting It Right Take a careful look at each page in your picture dictionary. Use this guide to revise the pages you are not happy with.

Question to Ask	How to Check	How to Revise
1. Do the signs on each page have the same job?	Read one sign, then check to make sure the other signs have the same job.	Replace a sign if it doesn't go with the other signs.
2. Does the picture help others understand what each sign means?	Have a partner tell you what each sign means.	Add a drawing or photo to your page that will help others understand.
3. Does each sign look real?	Compare each sign to your field trip notes.	Change the wording of your sign. Change the shape or color.
4. Does your caption explain the signs?	Check that the caption describes all of the signs.	Reword the caption.

4. Presenting It Share your work with your classmates.

❶ Form a group with classmates that visited different places.

I visited the mall!

I took the bus around town.

I took a walk around school!

My older brother took me on the freeway.

❷ Show each page in your book to the group. Read the signs and captions aloud.

❸ Be sure that each person in your group understands what each sign means.

❹ Ask for feedback from your classmates.

I can understand what each sign means!

Your English was perfect.

Your signs look real!

1. On Assignment Symbols are often used instead of words on signs. Work with your classmates. Make a poster that shows common symbols used in the community and explain what each symbol means.

❶ Begin by matching each of the following symbols from school with the correct word below.

a.

b.

c.

d.

e.

f.

g.

h.

i.

____f____ 1. library   _____ 6. phone

_____ 2. boys' bathroom   _____ 7. stairway

_____ 3. nurse's office   _____ 8. lost and found

_____ 4. cafeteria   _____ 9. gym

_____ 5. girls' bathroom

❷ Now walk or ride around your community. Draw the symbols you see in a notebook.

❸ Share and compare the symbols you have with those collected by your classmates. Choose the most common symbols from your community.

❹ Place the symbols neatly in rows on a separate piece of paper.

❺ Write a caption that explains each symbol. Your caption should be short and easy to read quickly.

 **SHARED READING** Listen to the poem "NO," by Shel Silverstein. Read along as you listen. Then, as a class, practice reading the poem aloud.

LET'S TALK Answer the following questions.

1. Name one "No" sign that you've seen before.
2. Name one "No" sign that you've never seen before.
3. Why is the poem funny?

ABOUT THE AUTHOR

Shel Silverstein was born in Chicago and died in 1999. He wrote nearly twenty-five books, published in 30 different languages. *Where the Sidewalk Ends*, *A Light in the Attic*, and *Falling Up* are three of his most famous collections of poetry and drawings.

No smoking
No spitting
No loitering
No littering
No drinking
No eating
No parking
No speeding
No fishing
No floating
No swimming
No boating
No surfing
No hiking
No hunting
No biking
No running
No skipping
No skinny-dipping
No volleyball players
No spray can sprayers
No fly rod casters
No boom box blasters
No trash leavers
No frisbee heavers

HEY—
IT DIDN'T SAY NO BEAVERS.

Source: *Falling Up* by Shel Silverstein

a spray can sprayer

a fly rod caster

a frisbee heaver

This Is My Web Page

Read...

■ Web pages written by students your age. Find out what other students are like and what they like to do.

Link to Literature

■ An autobiography poem written by a student.

Objectives:

Reading:
■ Understanding sentences expressing personal information
■ Understanding personal Web pages
■ Strategy: Using pictures to predict
■ Literature: Responding to poetry

Writing:
■ Creating a personal Web page
■ Putting information into categories
■ Using art and fonts to make writing interesting

Vocabulary:
■ Recognizing compound words
■ Learning words related to sports, recreation, and hobbies

Listening/Speaking:
■ Understanding a simple conversation
■ Listening to definitions and descriptions of things
■ Asking and answering questions
■ Giving personal information

Grammar:
■ Using complete sentences

Spelling and Phonics:
■ Pronouncing words with the pattern *o* + consonant + *e*

BEFORE YOU BEGIN

Talk with your classmates.

1. Whose Web page is this? Who created this Web page?
2. What do you know about Timo? Help your teacher make a list.
3. Where do you find Web pages?

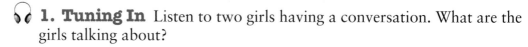

A CONNECTING TO YOUR LIFE

🎧 **1. Tuning In** Listen to two girls having a conversation. What are the girls talking about?

☐ people in their family   ☐ both of their boyfriends   ☐ things one of them likes to do

2. Talking It Over
Look at the pictures and descriptions below. Walk around your classroom and find one person for each description. Write the person's name on the line.

Find someone who...

...was born in January.

1. _____

...comes from Asia.

2. _____

...likes hip-hop music.

3. _____

...likes the color pink.

4. _____

...plans to go to college.

5. _____

...likes to swim.

6. _____

...is good at soccer.

7. _____

...gets good grades.

8. _____

Read the title of this unit. What do you think the unit is probably about? Check (✓) the correct answer.

_____ 1. It's about learning how to write about ourselves for a Web page.

_____ 2. It's about learning to use the Internet.

_____ 3. It's about learning how to write e-mail messages.

B GETTING READY TO READ

1. Learning New Words Read the sentences below. Try to figure out the meanings of the underlined words.

1. "Come in! It's nice to see you. <u>Welcome</u> to my home!"
2. *Funny Home Videos* makes me laugh. I <u>enjoy</u> watching that show.
3. Zaida watches *Funny Home Videos* every week. It's her <u>favorite</u> TV show.
4. Juan builds model cars every day after school. It's his <u>hobby.</u>
5. Stefan wants to help sick people. His <u>goal</u> is to be a doctor one day.
6. We know what happened yesterday, but nobody knows what will happen in the <u>future</u>.
7. Tran will <u>graduate</u> from high school in June. Then he will go to college.
8. Lori always gets A's and B's. She is a <u>successful</u> student.

Match each word on the left with the correct definition on the right.

1. welcome	a. good at what you do
2. enjoy	b. any time after right now
3. favorite	c. something you hope to do one day
4. hobby	d. a friendly greeting when someone comes to visit
5. goal	e. liked better than anything else
6. future	f. to finish high school, college, or some other educational program
7. graduate	g. to like doing something
8. successful	h. an activity you do for fun, usually by yourself

2. Talking It Over Complete the chart below. Then work in a small group. Talk about your life today and what you hope your life will be like in the future.

	Today	Ten Years from Now
Where I live		
What I do every day		
My favorite things		

C READING TO LEARN   Personal Web Pages

READING STRATEGY
Using Pictures to Make Predictions: When you see pictures and words together, the pictures can help you guess what the words will be about.

1. Before You Read Look at Keith's Web page. What does the picture tell you about Keith?

2. Let's Read Read about Keith. Do you like any of the same things?

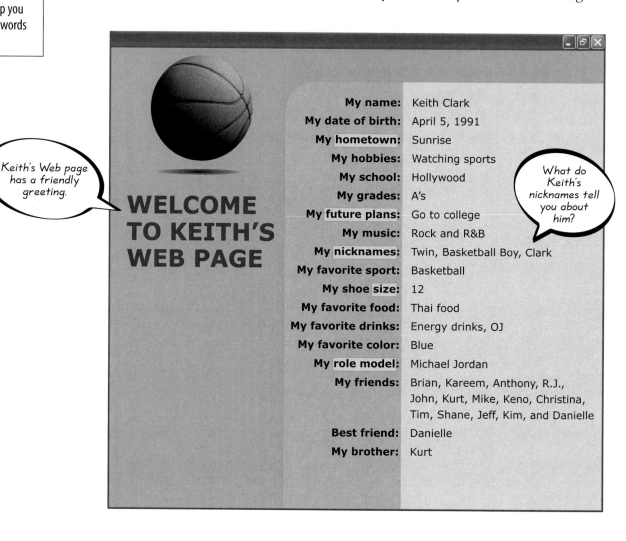

Keith's Web page has a friendly greeting.

What do Keith's nicknames tell you about him?

WELCOME TO KEITH'S WEB PAGE

My name:	Keith Clark
My date of birth:	April 5, 1991
My hometown:	Sunrise
My hobbies:	Watching sports
My school:	Hollywood
My grades:	A's
My future plans:	Go to college
My music:	Rock and R&B
My nicknames:	Twin, Basketball Boy, Clark
My favorite sport:	Basketball
My shoe size:	12
My favorite food:	Thai food
My favorite drinks:	Energy drinks, OJ
My favorite color:	Blue
My role model:	Michael Jordan
My friends:	Brian, Kareem, Anthony, R.J., John, Kurt, Mike, Keno, Christina, Tim, Shane, Jeff, Kim, and Danielle
Best friend:	Danielle
My brother:	Kurt

hometown—the place you come from

future plans—what you want to do when you are older

nickname—a name your friends call you

size—how big or small something is

role model—a person you want to be like

3. Unlocking Meaning

❶ Finding the Main Idea Choose the sentence that best describes Keith. Check (✓) the correct answer.

_____ 1. He is a college student who likes computers.

_____ 2. He is an unhappy person.

_____ 3. He is a high school student with many interests.

❷ Finding Details Read the sentences about Keith. Write _T_ for True or _F_ for False.

_____ 1. He is a good student.

_____ 2. He likes country music.

_____ 3. His favorite sport is football.

_____ 4. He has very small feet.

_____ 5. He loves Thai food.

_____ 6. He has a lot of friends.

_____ 7. He has a younger sister.

❸ Think about It Work with a partner. Complete the chart below. There is a sentence about Keith in each part. Use information on Keith's Web page to support each sentence.

He's good at sports. His favorite sport is basketball.	He's popular.
He's a good student.	He's like many other teenagers.

❹ Before You Move On What do you know about your own name? Find out. Be ready to share with your classmates.

1. Who gave you your name?
2. Why did they choose your name?
3. Does your name mean anything special?

4. Do you have nicknames at home?
5. Do you like your name?
6. If you could choose another name, what would it be? Why?

D WORD WORK

1. Word Detective Two words can sometimes be put together to form a new word. The new word is called a *compound word*. It has its own meaning: **home + town = hometown**

Look at these names for sports and activities. Find the smaller words in each compound word. What does each small word mean?

basketball	skydiving	weightlifting
football	softball	horseback riding

2. Word Study Some compound words are one word. Some are two words. Match each example in this chart with the correct type of compound word.

_b_	1. roller skates	a.	One word
_____	2. handball	b.	Two words
_____	3. baseball		
_____	4. running shorts		
_____	5. eyeball		

SPELLING AND PHONICS:
To do this activity, go to page 183.

3. Word Play Work with a partner. Think about the words in the box. Is each word a sport or a hobby? Complete the chart below. You can use your dictionary.

stamp collecting	windsurfing	bird watching
scuba diving	needlepoint	water-skiing
snowboarding	model building	woodworking

Sports / Hobbies

Sports require physical skill. They often have rules.

You often do hobbies by yourself, just for fun.

E GRAMMAR   Complete Sentences

1. Listen Up Listen to each sentence. Point your thumb up 👍 if it sounds correct. Point your thumb down 👎 if it sounds wrong.

1. I student.
2. My name Stefan.
3. I am in the ninth grade.

4. I am learning English.
5. Born in Poland.
6. Am sixteen years old.

2. Learn the Rule A sentence has to have certain things to be complete. Read the following rules for complete sentences. Then repeat Activity 1.

COMPLETE SENTENCES
1. A complete sentence has a subject and a complement. The subject is the person or thing that is doing or experiencing something. The **complement** finishes the idea. It identifies what the subject is doing or experiencing.
Maria **is sixteen years old.**   *Juan* **comes from Mexico.**
2. Every complement has a verb.
Maria **is sixteen years old.**   *Juan* **comes from Mexico.**

3. Practice the Rule Work with a partner. Tell a classmate about yourself using the following questions. Speak in complete sentences.

1. What is your name?
2. How old are you?
3. Where do you go to school?
4. Who is your best friend?
5. What grade are you in?
6. What is your favorite hobby?

F | BRIDGE TO WRITING   Personal Web Pages

READING STRATEGY
Using Pictures to Make Predictions: When you see pictures and words together, the pictures can help you guess what the words will be about.

1. Before You Read Personal Web pages often include personal profiles. Look at the picture below. Who do you think wrote the profiles at the bottom of the page for a Web site?

☐ a teacher
☐ a student
☐ a special class or club

2. Let's Read Read what these students say about themselves. Which person is most like you?

1 Darryl

I enjoy singing and am currently in the chorus.

I enjoy sports such as basketball and football.

My goals for the future are to graduate high school and attend a good college.

2 Rachel

I am on the honor roll.

My favorite subjects are world history and personal living.

My favorite hobbies are doing hair, exercising, listening to music, and playing basketball.

My goal for the future is to live a happy life and to be successful in the job I have.

3 Steven

My favorite subject in school is math because I will need math in the future.

My hobbies are fishing and riding bikes.

My goal for the future is to become an auto wholesaler.

chorus—a group of people who sing together

attend—to go to a class or school regularly

honor roll—a list recognizing students who get all A's and B's

personal living—a class that teaches you skills for everyday life

exercising—doing activities that make you strong and healthy

auto wholesaler—someone who sells cars

3. Making Content Connections Look at the students' profiles again. Complete the columns for Darryl, Rachel, and Steven in the chart below. Then, write your name at the top of the fourth column and add information about yourself.

	Darryl	Rachel	Steven	_____
What does this student like about school?	chorus			
What are this person's favorite hobbies or sports?				
What is this person's goal for the future?				

4. Expanding Your Vocabulary Work with a partner. Complete the chart below. Put each word in the box in the correct column.

Favorite Activities Word Bank

skateboarding	sailing	swimming	sewing
hiking	tennis	playing checkers	surfing
stamp collecting	jogging	biking	painting
camping	fishing	golf	bowling

	By Myself	With a Friend
Indoors		
Outdoors		

G | WRITING CLINIC

1. Think about It What is a personal Web page like? Explain.

☐ an imaginary story   ☐ a true life story   ☐ a movie or play

2. Focus on Organization

❶ Fold a sheet of paper in half lengthwise and then fold it again to create a chart with four parts. Label each part like the following example.

1. Information about Keith	2. Friends and Family
3. School	4. Favorite Things

❷ Look at Keith's Web page again. Put the information from Keith's Web page into the chart you've created. Make sure you include everything.

1. Information about Keith *Name: Keith Clark.* *Date of birth: April 5, 1991.*	2. Friends and Family *Brother: Kurt*
3. School	4. Favorite Things

❸ Rewrite Keith's Web page on a separate piece of paper. Use complete sentences with bullets. Use the model as an example.

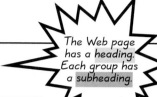

The Web page has a heading. Each group has a subheading.

Welcome to Keith's Web Page

About Me
• My name is Keith Clark.
• I was born April 5, 1991.

Some of My Favorite Things

My Friends and Family

My School

3. Focus on Style Web pages often use photos or art to describe a person. Which of these pictures would *you* add to Keith's Web page? Why? Circle your answers.

1.

2.

3.

4.

5.

6.

7.

8.

9.

H WRITER'S WORKSHOP   Personal Web Pages

Create your own "personal Web page." Your Web page will have three parts:

- a greeting and logo ————————— *Welcome to My Web Page!*

- a photograph or drawing of yourself

- information about yourself

————— *About me*

1. Getting It Out

❶ Fold a sheet of paper in half and then in half again to create four parts. What information do you want others to know from your Web page? Put your ideas in groups.

1. Information about Me *Name: Miguel Hernandez*	2. My Friends and Family
3. My School	4. My Favorite Things

❷ Decide what information about you is interesting. Share it with a partner.

My favorite sports are baseball and soccer.

My name is Miguel.

I have two sisters and one brother.

I'm a ninth grader at Kennedy Middle School.

Each "welcome" uses letters with different shapes, sizes, and colors.

❸ Think about your welcome. Which style do you like best? Why?

a.

Miguel's Web Page

b.

Here's Miguel!

c.

Meet Miguel

d.

Welcome to Miguel's Web Page!

❹ Look for a photo of yourself. Or draw your own portrait.

2. Getting It Down

❶ Make an outline like this. Use words and phrases that give information about you.

Welcome: _____

About Me   My Favorite Things
Name: Miguel Hernandez
Born in Mexico

My Friends and Family

---

❷ Turn your words into sentences.

About Me

My name is Miguel.
I was born in Mexico.

MINI-LESSON

Using Periods:
Put a period at the end of a sentence.

My favorite food is pizza.
Tran is my best friend.

■ ■ ■

❸ Here is the first part of Miguel's Web page:

Miguel's page has a welcome and a picture.

Welcome to Miguel's Web Page!

About Me
- My name is Miguel.
- I come from Mexico.
- I'm in the ninth grade.

My Friends and Family
- I have two sisters and one brother.
- I have a dog named Chipper.
- Tran is my best friend.

My Favorite Things
- My favorite sports are baseball and soccer.
- My favorite hobby is stamp collecting.
- My favorite food is pizza.

He puts the information in groups.

Miguel uses complete sentences.

3. Getting It Right Take a careful look at your Web page. Use this guide to revise your writing.

Question to Ask	How to Check	How to Revise
1. Will other students want to read my Web page?	Show your greeting to a partner. Ask if it is interesting.	Add a picture or change the size, shape, or color of the letters and words.
2. Is the information in groups?	Look at each group and make sure the information goes together.	Move some information to a different group.
3. Do I tell a lot about myself?	Make sure each group has two or three sentences.	Add more information about yourself to each group.
4. Do I use complete sentences?	Underline the subject and circle the complement in each sentence.	Add missing words to make complete sentences.

4. Presenting It Share your Web page design with the class. Take a "gallery walk" around the classroom and read your classmates' Web pages.

❶ Make a note-taking chart like this one. List the name of each classmate on the chart.

My Classmates	One Interesting Fact
Carlos	
Tran	
Lori	

❷ Help your teacher post the Web page designs along a bulletin board or wall.

❸ Read each Web page design. Take notes on your chart. Write one interesting fact about each person.

❹ Share one interesting fact you learned about a classmate with the class.

1. On Assignment Make a column graph that shows your favorite things.

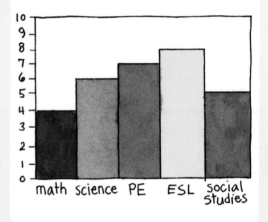

❶ Your teacher will give you six "answer cards." Label each card with one of these subjects:

Sport
Hobby
TV show
Food
School subject
Singer

❷ Fill out an answer card for each of the following questions:

What is your favorite sport?   What is your favorite food?

What is your favorite hobby?   What is your favorite subject in school?

What is your favorite TV show?   Who is your favorite singer?

❸ Divide up into six groups. Each group will get all the completed answer cards for *one* of the questions.

❹ Count up, or tally, how your class answered the question assigned to your group.

EXAMPLE:

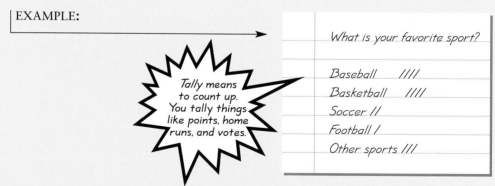

Tally means to count up. You tally things like points, home runs, and votes.

What is your favorite sport?

Baseball   ////
Basketball   ////
Soccer //
Football /
Other sports ///

❺ Make a column graph with the information from Step 4. Use a big piece of paper and colored markers. Share your graph with classmates.

2. Link to Literature

SHARED READING Read the autobiography poem written by Mikey L, who attends school in Edina, Minnesota.

LET'S TALK Answer the following questions.

1. What is one thing about Mikey that is just like you?
2. What is one thing about Mikey that is different from you?
3. What do you like about the poem? Why?

JUST FOR FUN Write your own autobiography poem. Use this planner to help you with organization.

1st line: Your first name only
2nd line: Three or four words that tell something about you
3rd line: Brother/Sister/Son/Daughter of _____
4th line: Who loves _____, _____, and _____
5th line: Who feels _____, _____, and _____
6th line: Who fears _____, _____, and _____
7th line: Who would like to see _____, _____, and _____
8th line: Your last name (or initial) only.

Mikey

Funny, nice, fun, and fast

Son of Nancy

Who loves popcorn, family, and the end of the school year

Who feels that school is too long, baseball is fun, and summer is too short

Who fears heights, breaking a bone, and lots of homework

Who would like to see the Vikings win the Super Bowl, school end, and New York

L

Source: edina.k12.mn.us

heights—high places

Vikings—Minnesota's football team

Super Bowl—the championship football game played every year in January

Read...

- Selections from *Looking at Maps and Globes* by Carmen Bredeson. Learn about maps and globes—and how to use them.

Link to Literature

- "Door Number Four," a poem by Charlotte Pomerantz.

Objectives:

Reading:
- Understanding maps and symbols
- Understanding captions that describe or explain
- Strategy: Connecting visuals with text
- Literature: Reading poetry

Writing:
- Making maps
- Labeling
- Choosing colors, fonts, and abbreviations
- Writing titles

Vocabulary:
- Learning names for places at school and in the community
- Recognizing antonyms
- Understanding basic map terminology

Listening/Speaking:
- Understanding a conversation
- Following directions for getting somewhere

Grammar:
- Making plural nouns

Spelling and Phonics:
- Spelling the /s/ sound as in *kiss* and *city*.

We're Lost!

BEFORE YOU BEGIN

Talk with your classmates.

1. Look at the picture. What are Juan and his brother doing? What is Juan looking at?

2. Read the caption. What is happening?

3. What are Juan and his brother saying to each other? Help your teacher write on the board the words they might be saying.

A **CONNECTING TO YOUR LIFE**

🎧 **1. Tuning In** Listen to the conversation between Juan and his brother. What is the problem?

☐ Juan is too young to drive.

☐ Juan forgot the address.

☐ Juan lost the map.

2. Talking It Over Work with a partner. Put the pictures and captions in the correct order. Then rewrite the sentences to tell where you live.

_____1_____ Jay lives in a house. His house is on Washington Street.

_____ Jay lives in the United States. The United States is on a continent: North America.

_____ Jay lives on Washington Street. Washington Street is in a neighborhoood.

_____ Jay lives in Columbus. Columbus is in the state of Nebraska.

_____ Jay lives in Nebraska. Nebraska is in a country: the United States.

_____ Jay lives in a neighborhood. His neighborhood is in the city of Columbus.

Read the title of this unit. What do you think the unit is probably about? Check (✓) the correct answer.

_____ 1. It's about people getting lost.

_____ 2. It's about knowing how to read maps and globes.

_____ 3. It's about following directions.

B GETTING READY TO READ

1. Learning New Words Read the sentences below. Try to figure out the meanings of the underlined words.

1. Tran doesn't know if Lori's house is north or south of his house. He doesn't know which <u>direction</u> her house is in.
2. A baseball, basketball, and volleyball are not square, they're <u>round</u>.
3. Zaida's house is like a box. It has a <u>flat</u> roof.
4. When you throw a football, it <u>curves</u> in the air.
5. Venus and Mars are planets. The <u>Earth</u> is a planet, too.
6. Jorge takes the bus to school. He can't walk there because he lives two <u>miles</u> away.
7. Miguel's dog Chipper has short legs. He is only one <u>foot</u> tall.
8. Chipper has a very short tail. It is only an <u>inch</u> long.

Match each word on the left with the correct definition on the right.

1. direction
2. round
3. flat
4. curve
5. Earth
6. mile
7. foot
8. inch

a. without any high or low areas
b. a U.S./English unit used to measure long distances (= 5,280 feet or 1.6 kilometers)
c. the way someone or something is facing, moving, or located in relation to you
d. a unit for measuring length (= 12 inches or 30.5 centimeters)
e. a unit for measuring short lengths (= $\frac{1}{12}$ of a foot or 2.54 centimeters)
f. the planet we live on
g. shaped like a ball or the letter "o"
h. to move like part of a circle

2. Talking It Over Work with a partner. On a separate piece of paper, make a list of places in the community you see every day or almost every day.

1. Before You Read Working in pairs, explain to a partner how to get from school to your house or apartment.

2. Let's Read Read the following information about maps. Look at and think about each picture as you read the caption.

Maps are flat drawings of areas of land that show us where to find different places.

1.

A map does not show exactly what something looks like.

2.

It is not like a photograph.

3.

Maps use symbols. Symbols are small pictures that mean different things. On this map, ▲▲ is the symbol for mountains; 🌳 is the symbol for parks.

4.
Map Legend
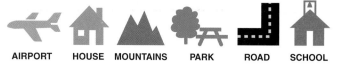
AIRPORT   HOUSE   MOUNTAINS   PARK   ROAD   SCHOOL
The map legend shows what each symbol means.

5.

There are many kinds of maps. A world map shows the whole Earth.

6.
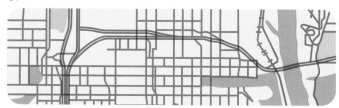
Some maps show just one town.

7.
You can draw a map to show a new friend how to get to your house.

8.
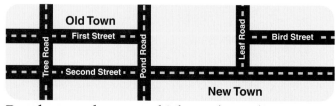
Road maps show us which road to take to get to another town.

9.

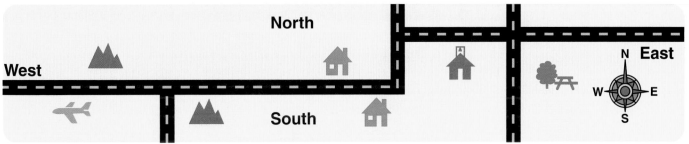

We use the directions north, south, east, and west to read a map. The top of a map is always north. The bottom of a map is south. East is to the right. West is to the left.

Source: *Looking at Maps and Globes* by Carmen Bredeson

3. Unlocking Meaning

❶ **Identifying the Purpose** Which phrase explains the main purpose of this unit? Check (✓) the correct answer.

_____ 1. to teach us how to go from one place to another

_____ 2. to teach us how to read maps

_____ 3. to teach us how to draw symbols

❷ **Finding Details** Complete the legend below. Match each symbol with a word.

a.

b.

c.

____*e*____ 1. sports stadium

_____ 2. hospital

_____ 3. airport

_____ 4. post office

d.

e.

f.

_____ 5. lake

_____ 6. library

❸ **Think about It** Work in four groups. Make a map for *one* quadrant, or ¼-part, of your classroom. Then put the four parts together.

❹ **Before You Move On** Draw a map that shows how to get from school to your home.

D WORD WORK

1. Word Detective Match each word on the left with the word on the right that means the opposite or almost the opposite.

1. round   a. west
2. top   b. little
3. east   c. flat
4. long   d. short
5. big   e. bottom

2. Word Study An antonym is a word with the opposite, or almost opposite, meaning of another word. Look at the examples below.

A map is <u>flat</u>.   A globe is <u>round</u>.
Canada is <u>north</u> of the U.S.   Mexico is <u>south</u> of the U.S.

3. Word Play Work with a partner. Write an antonym for each of the words below. Then write pairs of sentences using all the words. You can use your dictionary.

1. long	2. new	3. fast	4. narrow
short	_____	_____	_____
5. dark	6. hot	7. high	8. easy
_____	_____	_____	_____

1. _I have long hair. My brother has short hair._ _____

2. _____

3. _____

4. _____

5. _____

6. _____

7. _____

8. _____

SPELLING AND PHONICS:
To do this activity, go to page 183.

E GRAMMAR   Plural Nouns

1. Listen Up Listen to each sentence. Point your thumb up 👍 if it sounds correct. Point your thumb down 👎 if it sounds wrong.

👍👎 1. I'll have two cheeseburger.

👍👎 2. The library is two blocks away.

👍👎 3. I am taking five class at school.

👍👎 4. I can't see! I lost my glasses.

👍👎 5. This is a map.

👍👎 6. One bird is sitting on the fence and two birds are sitting in the tree.

2. Learn the Rule Adding one or two letters to nouns makes them plural. Read the rules for making singular nouns plural. Then repeat Activity 1.

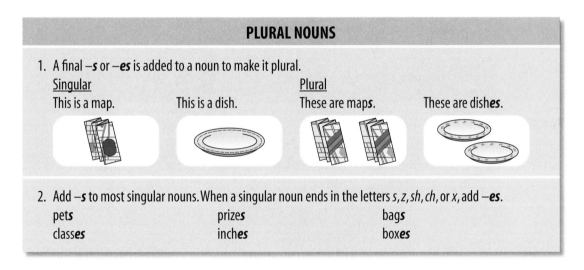

PLURAL NOUNS

1. A final **-s** or **-es** is added to a noun to make it plural.

Singular		Plural	
This is a map.	This is a dish.	These are map**s**.	These are dish**es**.

2. Add **-s** to most singular nouns. When a singular noun ends in the letters *s, z, sh, ch,* or *x,* add **-es**.

pet**s**   prize**s**   bag**s**

class**es**   inch**es**   box**es**

3. Practice the Rule Work with a partner. Complete each sentence with the plural form of the underlined noun.

1. Lori won a <u>prize</u>. Mario won two _____.
2. My favorite <u>class</u> is math. Juan's favorite _____ are PE and science.
3. One <u>car</u> is parked in the garage and two _____ are parked in the driveway.
4. Stefan has a <u>dog</u>. His friend William has a cat and two _____.
5. There's a <u>fox</u> in the yard. There are two more _____ in the woods.
6. I have four good _____. My best <u>friend</u> is Tran.

READING STRATEGY

Using Pictures:
When you see pictures and words together, the pictures can help you understand the meaning of the words.
■ ■ ■

F BRIDGE TO WRITING   Maps

1. Before You Read Look around your classroom. What kinds of maps do you see?

2. Let's Read Read more about maps. Use these pictures to help you understand each caption.

1.

Maps cannot show the real sizes of things. One hundred miles on Earth might take up just one inch on a map.

2.

The map scale shows us how many real miles are in one inch on the map. On this scale, one inch equals one mile.

3.

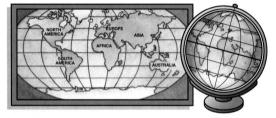

It is hard to show the round Earth on a flat map. A flat piece of paper does not curve. A round globe shows us how the world really looks. It curves like the Earth.

4.

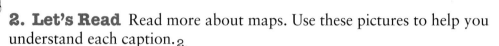

The top of the globe shows us the part of the Earth called the North Pole. The bottom of the globe shows us the South Pole.

5.

The imaginary line that wraps around the middle of the globe is called the equator. Find the United States on the globe. Is it above or below the equator?

6.

It is fun to find places on the globe. You can travel around the world with just your finger!

Source: *Looking at Maps and Globes* by Carmen Bredeson

equal—to be the same as

imaginary—not real

wrap around—to go all the way around

travel—to go places

3. Making Content Connections Draw a simple map that shows how to get from your house to a classmate's house. Your classmate should make the same map. Compare your maps. How are they the same? How are they different?

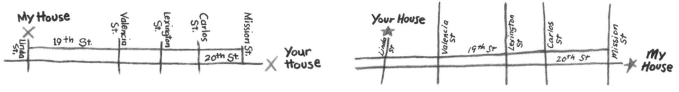

From my house to your house.   *From your house to my house.*

4. Expanding Your Vocabulary A map sometimes shows buildings and other landmarks. Match each item in the map below with its name.

__c__	1. library		_____	7. bakery
_____	2. hotel		_____	8. movie theater
_____	3. health club		_____	9. playground
_____	4. car dealership		_____	10. supermarket
_____	5. post office		_____	11. newsstand
_____	6. museum		_____	12. fast food restaurant

G | **WRITING CLINIC** | Maps

1. Think about It Where are three places you often find maps?

☐ in an atlas   ☐ in a novel   ☐ in your history textbook

☐ in a teen magazine   ☐ in the newspaper   ☐ on a CD cover

2. Focus on Organization

A route map shows how to get from one place to another. Look at this route map. The sentences below the map explain what the purpose of each part is.

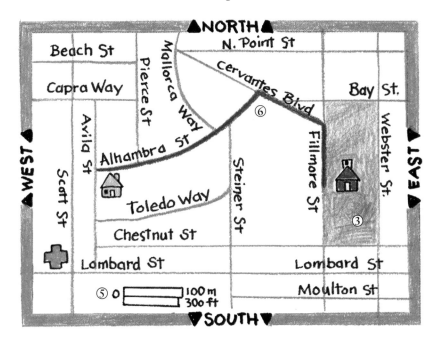

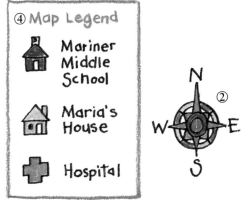

① The map has a title.

② A compass shows direction.

③ The map uses symbols.

④ A legend shows what the symbols mean.

⑤ The map shows the scale.

⑥ The route is easy to follow.

3. Focus on Style

❶ Many maps use colors, shapes, and lines to improve understanding. Colors can help show different places and routes. Look again at the map. What do you think the green area probably shows?

☐ a parking lot   ☐ a swimming pool   ☐ a park or sports field

Why is the route highlighted in purple? Talk with a partner.

❷ Which colors would you use on a map? Match each color on the left with a place on the right.

1. blue ■   a. a freeway, road, or street
2. green ■   b. a place with lots of snow
3. gray ■   c. a warm place with lots of sun (like a beach)
4. white □   d. a park or recreational area
5. red ■   e. water (an ocean, lake, or river)
6. yellow ▢   f. a place that gets little rain (like the desert)
7. brown ■   g. a fire station

❸ Maps often use symbols to show where buildings and landmarks are located. Match each building or landmark on the left with the correct symbol on the right.

1. airport   a.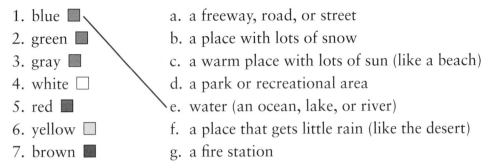

2. school   b.

3. mountain   c.

❹ Maps tell the names of streets and roads. They use a font, or print style, that is easy to read. Which of these do you think is the best font for a street map?

1. *Main Street*   3. *Main Street*
2. Main Street   4. **MAIN STREET**

❺ Maps also use abbreviations, or short forms of words, to name different types of streets. Match each abbreviation on the left with a full word on the right.

1. Blvd.   a. Street
2. Ave.   b. Road
3. Hwy.   c. Boulevard
4. Rd.   d. Avenue
5. St.   e. Highway

H | WRITER'S WORKSHOP   Maps

Imagine that you are a *cartographer*, or mapmaker. Create a class map book. Work with a partner.

1. Getting It Out

❶ Decide what kind of map you will make. Choose a small area to map out, one you can easily walk to.

❷ Gather the materials you will need.

1. sketchpad
2. sheet of chart paper or white construction paper
3. pencil
4. ruler
5. colored marking pens
6. calculator (optional)

❸ Walk around the area. Make a rough drawing as you walk.

Each block is about 250 steps. That's about 500 feet.

This is the library.

Estimate, or guess, sizes and distances by walking. Each step equals about two feet.

Write down the names of each street and label buildings and important places.

❹ Decide on the scale of your map.

The size of our map will be 10 inches by 12 inches. Each inch will equal 500 feet.

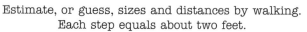

2. Getting It Down

❶ Use your rough drawing to lay out your map. Measure carefully. Use a pencil so you can erase mistakes!

❷ Label streets, buildings, and other important places. Use symbols, if you wish.

❸ Add a legend to show what each symbol means.

❹ Add a bar to show the scale of your map.

❺ Give your map a title.

Here is the map that Juan and Jorge made of their school.

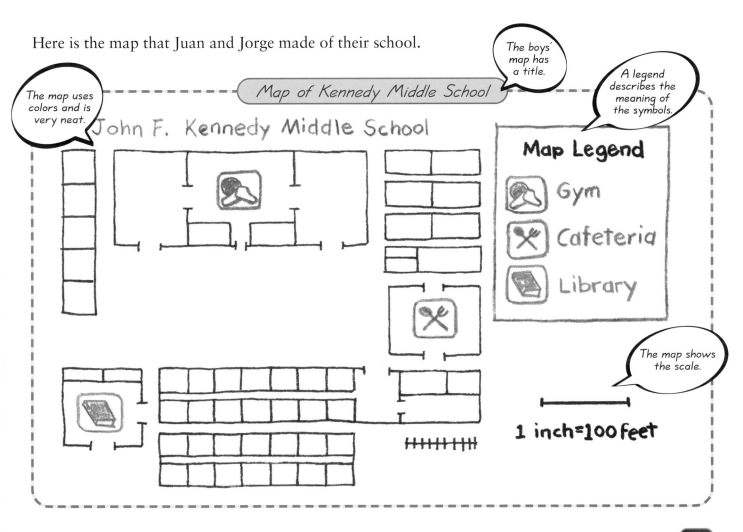

The boys' map has a title.

A legend describes the meaning of the symbols.

The map uses colors and is very neat.

Map of Kennedy Middle School

John F. Kennedy Middle School

Map Legend

Gym

Cafeteria

Library

The map shows the scale.

1 inch = 100 feet

3. Getting It Right

❶ Take a careful look at your map. Use this guide to help you revise your work.

Question to Ask	How to Check	How to Revise
1. Does our map have a title?	Ask your partner to read the title aloud.	Add a title that begins, "Map of _____."
2. Is our map to scale?	Ask an adult, such as your teacher, if your map appears to be to scale.	Change the sizes of buildings or the lengths of streets. Add a scale bar to show what one inch equals.
3. Do we use symbols? If so, does our map have a legend?	Lightly circle each symbol in pencil.	Add symbols for common places. Include a legend.
4. Is our map accurate and easy to follow?	Ask other students if they understand your map.	Make changes, based on the feedback you get.

❷ Develop your final draft.

- Trace over pencil lines with marking pen
- Add color
- Make sure that your map is neatly drawn

4. Presenting It

❶ Share your map with your classmates.

❷ Ask for feedback.

Your map is neat and colorful.

Your map is easy to read.

Your map looks like it is drawn to scale.

❸ Compare your map with similar maps that your classmates made.

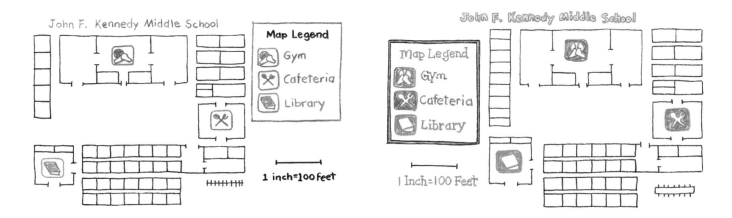

John F. Kennedy Middle School

Map Legend
🤸 Gym
✖ Cafeteria
📖 Library

1 inch=100 feet

John F. Kennedy Middle School

Map Legend
🤸 Gym
✖ Cafeteria
📖 Library

1 Inch=100 Feet

1. On Assignment Learn more about different types of maps. Look in the newspaper to find examples.

❶ Almost every issue of the newspaper has maps. How many different types of maps can you find? Find examples to share with classmates.

1.

Political maps show countries, states, and cities.

2.

Physical maps show natural features, like mountains, oceans, lakes, and rivers.

3.

Road maps show types of roads and where places are located.

4.

Weather maps show rain, sleet, and snow.

❷ Choose a map from a recent edition of your local newspaper. Show the map to your classmates and explain it to them.

This is a weather map.

What kind of map is it?

The map shows how much snow fell.

Why was this map in the newspaper?

The map is hard to read. It could be larger.

Is it a good map? Could it be better? How?

SHARED READING Read this poem about going to a friend's house. The poem has Indonesian words in it.

LET'S TALK Answer the following questions and do the activity.

1. Where does the poem take place—in the country or in the city?

2. The poem is about two friends. Do they speak the same language?

3. Match each Indonesian word on the left with an English word on the right.

1. teman	a. number
2. nomer	b. friend
3. empat	c. hush hush
4. pintu	d. four
5. diam-diam	e. door

Sometimes the same word is used in two different languages. Which word is the same or almost the same in both languages?

ABOUT THE AUTHOR

Charlotte Pomerantz was born in New York City, where she still lives. She is the author of many books for young people, including *Mangaboom*, *Here Comes Henny*, *Halfway to Your House*, and *Posy*.

Door Number Four
Charlotte Pomerantz

Above my uncle's grocery store
is a pintu,
is a door.
On the pintu
is a number,
nomer empat,
number four.
In the door
there is a key.
Turn it,
enter quietly,
Hush hush, diam-diam,
quietly.
There, in lamplight,
you will see
a friend,
teman,
a friend
who's me.

The meaning of the Indonesian word is always in the next line.

Source: *If I Had a Paka* by Charlotte Pomerantz

enter—to go in

lamplight—the light from a lamp

Mean and Lazy

Read...

- Selections from *The Meanest: Amazing Facts about Aggressive Animals* and *The Laziest: Amazing Facts about Lazy Animals* by Mymi Doinet.

Learn about animals who would rather bite than make friends and creatures that are the couch potatoes of the animal kingdom.

Link to Literature

- "Wild Animals," an alphabet poem written by students.

Objectives:

Reading:
- Understanding information about animals in texts and charts
- Strategy: Finding details
- Literature: Responding to poetry

Writing:
- Writing complete sentences
- Contributing a page to a class field guide
- Using adjectives to enliven writing
- Helping to write a class picture dictionary about animals
- Helping to create a class alphabet poem about animals

Vocabulary:
- Learning word groups: Size, height, and weight
- Learning names of wild animals

Listening/Speaking:
- Understanding an oral narrative
- Answering questions about information in a chart
- Telling about and describing animals
- Giving others feedback

Grammar:
- Understanding subject-verb agreement

Spelling and Phonics:
- Pronouncing words with the letter *a*

A Bengal tiger

BEFORE YOU BEGIN

Talk with your classmates.

1. Look at the picture. What do you see? What would you do if you met one of these animals?
2. Read the caption. What type of tiger is this?
3. What does the Bengal tiger look like? Help your teacher write a description.

1. Tuning In   Listen to the conversation. Eduardo and Brian are talking about a time when something exciting happened. What happened?

- ☐ They killed a huge snake.
- ☐ A snake almost killed them.
- ☐ They took a picture of a snake.

2. Talking It Over   How many of these animals do you recognize? Match the pictures with the names.

_____   1. Komodo dragon   _____   4. hippopotamus

_____   2. anaconda   _____   5. praying mantis

_____   3. cow   _____   6. cat

a.

b.

c.

d.

e.

f.

Talk with a partner. Decide which of these animals are *mean* and which animals are *lazy*.

Read the title of this unit. What do you think the unit is probably about? Check (✓) the correct answer.

_____   1. It's about kids you know who you don't like.

_____   2. It's about people who are mean to others.

_____   3. It's about animals that are scary and animals that sleep a lot.

B GETTING READY TO READ

1. Learning New Words Read the sentences below. Try to figure out the meanings of the underlined words.

1. Fred lives on Mansfield Street. His <u>address</u> is 4876 Mansfield Street.
2. Erik has very big feet. He wears a <u>size</u> 13 shoe.
3. An elephant is very heavy. It has the same <u>weight</u> as a truck.
4. My German shepherd is a big dog. He weighs almost 100 <u>pounds</u>.
5. Many people have golden retrievers. They're a popular <u>breed</u>.
6. Cats are pets that live indoors with people. They are <u>domestic</u> animals.

Match each word on the left with its correct definition on the right.

1. address   a. how heavy or how light something is
2. size   b. a unit used to measure weight (= 16 ounces or 454 grams)
3. weight   c. the street name and number where someone lives or works
4. pound   d. used to describe an animal that lives with people or works on a farm
5. breed
6. domestic   e. how big or how small something is
     f. a type of animal

2. Talking It Over Talk with a partner. Which of the animals below are good pets? Which are bad pets? Why?

1.

Goldfish

2.

A rabbit

3.

Baby alligators

4.

A chimpanzee

5.

A parakeet

6.
A cat

C **READING TO LEARN**   Field Guides

1. Before You Read Look at the pictures. Where do these animals mostly live?

☐ in the city   ☐ in the jungle   ☐ underneath houses

🎧 **2. Let's Read** Read about three animals. Underline details that show how the animals are scary. Which animal scares you the most?

9.5 is pronounced "nine point five."

1 Komodo Dragon

This gigantic lizard can swallow over six pounds
(2.7 kilograms) of meat in a minute.

Address: Indonesia

Size: Up to 9.5 feet (about 3 meters) long

Weight: Can reach weights greater than 300 pounds
(136 kilograms)

Favorite food: Wild boar and deer

2 Anaconda

This 450-pound snake can swallow a
7-foot-long (2.13-meter-long) caiman whole!

Address: Swamplands of the Amazon,
Guyana, the Orinoco basin of South America.

Size: From 10 to 30 feet (3 to 9 meters) long

Weight: From 440 to 506 pounds (200 to 230 kilograms)

Favorite food: Fish, tapirs, caimans, and any
animal that comes to the water to drink

3 Praying Mantis

Sometimes the female mantis
hugs her mate so tight, she pops his head
off ... then she eats his body!

Address: North America, southern Europe, Africa, Asia

Size: Male: From 1 to 4 inches (2.5 to 10 centimeters) long

Female: From 2 to 6 inches (5 to 15 centimeters) long

Favorite food: Butterflies, flies, and other insects

Source: *The Meanest: Amazing Facts about Aggressive Animals* by Mymi Doinet

gigantic—very large

swallow—to make food go down your throat

greater than—more than

wild boar—a type of wild pig

caiman—a type of crocodile

swamplands—land that is covered with water

tapir—an animal with a heavy body and short legs

hug—to use arms or legs to squeeze

mate—the partner of an animal

pop—to break

3. Unlocking Meaning

❶ Identifying the Main Idea What are the reading selections about? Check (✓) the correct answer.

_____ 1. animals that eat people

_____ 2. animals that attack, or hurt and kill, other animals

_____ 3. animals that are all very large

❷ Finding Details Read the sentences below. Write *T* for True or *F* for False.

_____ 1. The Komodo dragon is an insect.

_____ 2. The Komodo dragon is very large.

_____ 3. The Komodo dragon weighs more than most people.

_____ 4. The anaconda is a large snake.

_____ 5. The anaconda eats butterflies and other insects.

_____ 6. The anaconda lives near water.

_____ 7. The praying mantis is an insect.

_____ 8. The praying mantis lives mostly in South America.

_____ 9. The male praying mantis kills and eats the female.

❸ Think about It Talk with a partner. Which of the animals you read about is most likely to harm or kill people? Why?

❹ Before You Move On Can you guess why the type of mantis in the picture is called the *praying* mantis?

D WORD WORK

1. Word Detective Look at the measurement chart below. Listen to the sentences. Point your thumb up 👍 if the sentence is right. Point your thumb down 👎 if it is wrong.

SPELLING AND PHONICS:
To do this activity, go to page 184.

2. Word Study It is sometimes helpful to learn words in groups. Look at the chart below for groups of words that describe size, length, and weight. Write three sentences using the information in the chart below.

EXAMPLE: *The thread snake is tiny.*

Measurement Word Groups			
	Size	Length	Weight
Thread snake	tiny	very short (3 inches or 7.6 centimeters)	very light (several ounces or between 100 and 200 grams)
Brown snake	small	short (9 to 12 inches or 22.9 to 30.5 centimeters)	light (less than a pound or half a kilogram)
Kingsnake	medium size	medium length (36 to 72 inches or 91.4 to 182.9 centimeters)	medium weight (2 to 3 pounds or 0.9 to 1.4 kilograms)
Boa constrictor	big/large	long (over 8 feet or 2.4 meters)	heavy (30 pounds or 13.6 kilograms)
Anaconda	huge/gigantic	very long (up to 30 feet or 9.1 meters)	very heavy (up to 500 pounds or 227 kilograms)

3. Word Play Work with a partner. Write three sentences about your own life using the words in the word families.

E GRAMMAR   Subject-Verb Agreement

1. Listen Up Listen to each sentence. Point your thumb up 👍 if it sounds correct. Point your thumb down 👎 if it sounds wrong.

👍👎 1. Dogs chases cats.

👍👎 2. My cat loves to eat mice.

👍👎 3. Anacondas can kills alligators.

👍👎 4. Anacondas live in South America.

👍👎 5. A Komodo dragon weigh over 300 pounds.

👍👎 6. The praying mantis like to eat butterflies.

2. Learn the Rule In a good sentence, the subject and the verb must agree. Read the following rules to learn how to make present tense verbs agree with the subjects. Then do Activity 1 again.

SUBJECT-VERB AGREEMENT WITH PRESENT TENSE VERBS

1. When the subject of a sentence is a singular noun (praying mantis, alligator), the verb ends in -s or -es.
   *A female praying mantis **eats** its mate.*
   *The anaconda **squeezes** its victim to death.*

2. When the subject is a plural noun (anacondas), the verb does not end in -s or -es.
   *Anacondas **live** in South America.*

3. When *can* comes before the verb, the verb does not end in -s or -es.
   *An anaconda can **swallow** a human in one bite!*

3. Practice the Rule Look at the sentences below. Circle the correct form of each verb.

1. The Komodo dragon (live/lives) in Indonesia.
2. Komodo dragons (kill/kills) other animals.
3. The anaconda (reach/reaches) 30 feet in length.
4. It (weigh/weighs) up to 500 pounds.
5. Baby anacondas can (eat/eats) baby birds.
6. The female praying mantis (hug/hugs) her mate to death.
7. The praying mantis can (change/changes) color from green to brown.

Mean and Lazy 81

F BRIDGE TO WRITING   Field Guides

READING STRATEGY
Finding Details:
You can look for details to answer a specific question about a reading passage.
■ ■ ■

1. Before You Read Look at the pictures below. What do you notice about these animals?

🎧 **2. Let's Read** Read about three "lazy" animals. Underline details that show how the animals are lazy.

1 Cow

Lying in a pasture or on a bed of hay, the cow chews its cud 10 to 12 hours each day. Then it sleeps through the night!

Address: Farms all over the world

Size: About 4.5 feet (1.4 meters) from the shoulders down

Weight: From 650 to 2,000 pounds (300 to 900 kilograms), depending upon the breed

Favorite food: In summer, fresh grass, clover, and dandelions; in winter, hay and grain

2 Hippopotamus

The hippopotamus rests all day submerged in the water ... to keep from getting sunburned!

Address: Rivers and lakes of Africa

Size: From 11 to 12 feet (3.4 to 3.7 meters) long

Weight: Male: About 3,500 to 7,000 pounds (1,590 to 3,180 kilograms)
Female: About 1,400 to 5,160 pounds (635 to 2,300 kilograms)

Favorite food: Herbs and other plants

3 Cat

The domestic cat sleeps for 18 out of every 24 hours, and yawns at least 40 times a day!

Address: North America, South America, Europe, Africa, Asia, and Australia

Size: Up to 3.5 feet (1 meter) long from the tip of the nose to the tip of the tail

Weight: From 4 to 16 pounds (1.8 to 7.3 kilograms), depending upon the breed

Favorite food: Meat, fish, and poultry

Source: *The Laziest: Amazing Facts about Lazy Animals* by Mymi Doinet

pasture—grassland where cattle feed

cud—food already eaten once, then brought back into the mouth

clover—a grasslike plant with three round leaves

dandelion—a plant with tiny yellow flowers

grain—crops like corn, wheat, or rice

submerged—under water

sunburned—used to describe skin that is burned by the sun

herb—a plant used for flavor in cooking

yawn—to open your mouth wide when you are sleepy

poultry—birds like chickens and turkeys

3. Making Content Connections Work with a partner. Choose one mean animal and one lazy animal. Compare the two. How are they different? Complete the chart below.

	Mean Animal: _____	Lazy Animal: _____
What is one interesting fact about it?		
Where does it live?		
How big does it get?		
What does it eat?		

4. Expanding Your Vocabulary Match each animal name on the left with a picture on the right. Write the letters on the lines.

_h_   1. giraffe

_____   2. tiger

_____   3. leopard

_____   4. lion

_____   5. gorilla

_____   6. dingo

_____   7. orangutan

_____   8. rhinoceros

a.

e.

b.

f.

c.

g.

d.

h.

G | WRITING CLINIC   Field Guides

1. Think about It Who would probably like to read a field guide?

☐ a scientist   ☐ an airline pilot   ☐ a police officer
☐ a lawyer   ☐ a student   ☐ someone interested in nature

2. Focus on Organization

❶ A field guide often gives us information about an animal.

①
③
④
⑤

1 The Komodo Dragon   ②

This gigantic lizard can swallow over six pounds (2.7 kilograms) of meat in a minute.

Address: Indonesia

Size: Up to 9.5 feet (about 3 meters) long

Weight: Can reach weights greater than 300 pounds (136 kilograms)

Favorite food: Wild boar and deer

---

① Here is the name of the animal.
② Here is a picture of the animal
③ Here is an amazing fact about the animal.
④ This tells where the animal lives.
⑤ Here is basic information about the animal.

❷ Answer these questions by writing the numbers from the Anaconda field guide below on the lines.

___4___   1. What part tells where the animal lives?

_____   2. What part shows what the animal looks like?

_____   3. What part tells us the name of the animal?

_____   4. What part gives the reader basic information about the animal?

_____   5. What part tells us an amazing fact about the animal?

①
③
④
⑤

The Anaconda   ②

This 450-pound snake can swallow a 7-foot-long (2.13-meter-long) caiman whole!

Address: Swamplands of the Amazon, Guyana, the Orinoco basin of South America.

Size: From 10 to 30 feet (3 to 9 meters) long

Weight: From 440 to 506 pounds (200 to 230 kilograms)

Favorite food: Fish, tapirs, caimans, and any animal that comes to the water to drink

3. Focus on Style

❶ Adjectives help make your writing interesting. Circle the adjective in each of these sentences.

1. The Komodo dragon is a gigantic lizard.
2. The anaconda wraps its large body around its victim.

1. ferocious
2. hungry
3. ~~tiny~~
4. colorful
5. ugly
6. huge

❷ Complete the following sentences with words from the pictures above.

1. The _____*tiny*_____ mosquito bites people.
2. The _____ lion is king of the jungle.
3. The _____ elephant weighs several tons.
4. A _____ shark sometimes kills people.
5. The vampire bat has a very _____ face.
6. The mandrill is a _____ animal.

H WRITER'S WORKSHOP   Field Guides

Imagine that your class is writing a field guide about the *meanest* animals on Earth. Make a page for the book.

1. Getting It Out

❶ Choose an animal to write about. Look at the pictures below for ideas or choose another creature.

1 Great White Shark

Facts: Loves to eat meat

Sometimes eats other sharks

Lives in the Pacific Ocean and Atlantic Ocean

Is 12 to 21 feet (3.7 to 6.4 meters) long

Weighs about 5,000 pounds (2,300 kilograms)

Eats seals, sea turtles, and dolphins

2 Vampire Bat

Facts: Drinks blood at night from sleeping animals (must have blood every 48 hours)

Lives in Mexico and South America

Is 2.5 to 4 inches (6.4 to 10 centimeters) long

Very light: weighs 0.5 to 1.75 ounces (14 to 50 grams)

Loves the blood of cattle (cows and bulls)

3 Crocodile

Facts: One of the world's most dangerous reptiles

Lives in rivers, lakes, and bays

Can be as long as 25 feet (7.6 meters)

Loves to eat humans

Has very powerful jaws

Usually drowns its victims

4 Bengal Tiger

Facts: Teeth are like knives and over 3 inches (7.6 centimeters) long

Hunts at night

Lives in India, Nepal, and Myanmar

Almost 10 feet (3 meters) long

Male weighs 375 to 550 pounds (170 to 250 kilograms)
Female weighs 220 to 330 pounds (100 to 150 kilograms)

Eats deer, buffalo, pigs, and baby elephants

Source: *The Meanest: Amazing Facts about Aggressive Animals* by Mymi Doinet

❷ Take out a sheet of paper. Print the name of the animal you chose at the top. Fold the paper in half and then in half again to create four sections. Number each section and copy the questions from the chart below.

Here is what Graciela wrote. What do you think?

Mosquito

1. What is one amazing fact about the animal?
The female flaps her wings 800 times a second when looking for skin to bite.

2. Where does it live?
It lives in every part of the world, especially in places with warm weather.

3. How big/heavy is it?
It's 0.16 to 0.4 inches long.

4. What is its favorite food?
Fresh blood!

❸ Draw a picture of the animal or cut out a photograph from a magazine.

❹ Look at the map below. Shade in the places where your animal lives. Print the name of each shaded-in place on your map.

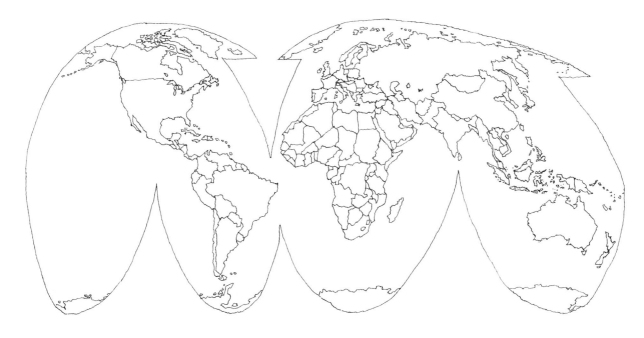

2. Getting It Down

❶ Copy the plan below and create an outline about your animal.

Name:

One amazing fact:

Address:

Size:

Weight:

Favorite food:

MINI-LESSON

Using Colons:
Use a colon to introduce information in a category.

Favorite food:
fresh blood

---

❷ Now turn your outline into a page for the field guide. Add a picture and map. Here is what Graciela wrote about the mosquito.

Graciela names the animal and includes a picture.

She tells an amazing fact about the mosquito. She uses a complete sentence.

Mosquito

Bzzzz! The female mosquito flaps her wings 800 times per second as she flies around looking for fresh blood.

Address:

North America; South America; Europe;

Asia; Africa; Australia; Pacific Islands

Places in the world with warm weather, water, and animals with blood

She tells us important facts about the mosquito.

Size:

From 0.16 to 0.4 inches long

Favorite Food:

Male: Flower nectar

Female: Fresh blood

Graciela includes a map.

nectar—sweet liquid in flowers

3. Getting It Right Now take a careful look at what you have written. Use this guide to revise your page.

Question to Ask	How to Check	How to Revise
1. Does my page name the animal?	<u>Underline</u> the name of the animal.	Add a title with the animal's name to your page.
2. Do I use a complete sentence to tell an amazing fact?	Put a check mark (✓) in front of the sentence that tells an amazing fact.	Add a verb or direct object to your sentence to make it complete.
3. Does the verb agree with the subject?	Reread the rule for subject-verb agreement on page 81.	Add -s or -es to the verb, if you need to.
4. Does my page have a picture and map?	Put a star (★) next to the picture and a check mark (✓) next to the map.	Add a picture and/or map if you don't have them.

4. Presenting It Share your page for the field guide with your classmates.

❶ Begin by showing your page and saying which animal you chose to write about.

❷ Read your page aloud. Read slowly and speak clearly.

❸ Ask if anyone has any questions.

❹ Tell your classmates what you like about their reports.

1. On Assignment Make a class picture dictionary of animals.

❶ Help your teacher make a list of animals from A to Z. The following chart will help you with some of the more difficult animals to name.

A: anaconda

B: _____

C: cat, cow

D: _____

E: eel

F: _____

G: _____

H: hippopotamus

I: _____

J: _____

K: Komodo dragon

L: _____

M: mosquito

N: _____

O: _____

P: _____

Q: quetzal

R: _____

S: _____

T: _____

U: unicorn

V: vulture

W: _____

X: xenops

Y: yak

Z: _____

A quetzal

A xenops

A yak

❷ Choose a letter from the alphabet. Find as many names as you can for animals that begin with this letter. ⟶

antelope

aardvark

anaconda

aardvark

anaconda

antelope

❸ Make a page for the animal dictionary. Put your animals in alphabetical order.

❹ Make a page for each animal. Find a picture of each animal or draw your own picture. Label the pictures with the animal names.

❺ Put the pages in alphabetical order and attach them to each other to make a book.

2. Link to Literature

SHARED READING Read this alphabet poem written by students.

LET'S TALK Answer the following questions and do the activity.

1. Why is this poem called an alphabet poem?
2. What does each line in the poem begin with?
3. Find three adjectives in the poem.

JUST FOR FUN Write a class alphabet poem about animals.

1. Look again at the page you made for your class picture dictionary.
2. Choose one animal. Write a sentence about the animal.
3. Place your line in the right place in the alphabet to make your class poem.

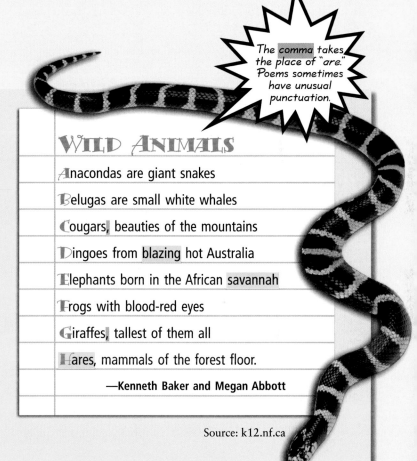

The comma takes the place of "are." Poems sometimes have unusual punctuation.

WILD ANIMALS

Anacondas are giant snakes

Belugas are small white whales

Cougars, beauties of the mountains

Dingoes from blazing hot Australia

Elephants born in the African savannah

Frogs with blood-red eyes

Giraffes, tallest of them all

Hares, mammals of the forest floor.

—Kenneth Baker and Megan Abbott

Source: k12.nf.ca

blazing—very hot

savannah—grassland

hare—a wild rabbit

You Can Cook!

Read...

- Recipes for every meal from *The Everything® Kids' Cookbook*. From quesadillas to s'mores—learn about all you need to have fun in the kitchen.

Link to Literature

- "A Recipe for Weather" by an unknown poet.

Objectives:

Reading:

- How-to instructions: Understanding recipes
- Strategy: Visualizing as you read
- Literature: Reading a recipe poem

Writing:

- Writing a recipe for a class cookbook
- Listing steps of a process in time order
- Writing interesting names for recipes

Vocabulary:

- Learning names of cooking utensils and ingredients
- Noticing words borrowed from other languages
- Recognizing compound words
- Idioms with food words

Listening/Speaking:

- Understanding the purpose of a conversation
- Explaining steps in a process
- Demonstrating a recipe

Grammar:

- Understanding prepositions that indicate location

Spelling and Phonics:

- Spelling the /k/ sound as in *king* and *cat*

Chef Miguel

BEFORE YOU BEGIN

Talk with your classmates.

1. Look at the picture. What is the boy doing?
2. Read the caption. Who is the cook?
3. What is happening? Help your teacher write sentences about the picture.

A CONNECTING TO YOUR LIFE

1. Tuning In Listen to the conversation between a woman and her son. What is the woman teaching her son to do?

☐ make a burrito ☐ use the microwave oven ☐ eat a burrito

2. Talking It Over

Work with a partner. Make a "Super Burrito"—the best burrito in the world!

List the ingredients you will put into your burrito. Share the list with your classmates.

beef   tortillas   cooked beans

sour cream   salsa   rice

shredded chicken   black olives   guacamole   shredded cheese

These are all ingredients. Ingredients are the things that go together to make a dish, or a food prepared in a certain way (like curry, egg rolls, or...burritos!)

Read the title of this unit. What do you think the unit is probably about? Check (✓) the correct answer.

_____ 1. It's about how people grow our foods.

_____ 2. It's about reading and writing *recipes*, or directions, for making different dishes.

_____ 3. It's about foods that are good for you and bad for you.

B GETTING READY TO READ

1. Learning New Words Match each cooking utensil in the picture with a description below.

_____b_____ 1. a machine used to heat food very quickly

_____ 2. a metal pan used to cook or bake food in the oven

_____ 3. a machine used to bake or broil food

_____ 4. tools used to measure small amounts

_____ 5. a sharp tool used to cut food into small pieces

_____ 6. a tool used to lift, turn, or flip pieces of food

_____ 7. a flat dish used to serve food on

_____ 8. a tool made of wood and used to stir or mix food together

_____ 9. a small, deep metal pan used to cook food on the stove

_____ 10. a cup used to measure large amounts of ingredients

a.

knife

b.

microwave oven

c.
oven

d.
plate

e.
measuring spoons

f.
wooden spoon

g.

glass measuring cup

h.

baking pan

i.

saucepan

j.

spatula

2. Talking It Over Match the items in the box with the recipes below. Write the names of the recipes on the lines.

Egg salad sandwich	Smoothie	Cookies	Tossed green salad

tbsp. = tablespoon, *tsp.* = teaspoon, and *oz.* = ounce.

Recipe #1: _____

1 cup orange juice   ½ cup frozen peaches

1 banana   ½ cup frozen berries

Recipe #2: _____

2 hard boiled eggs   2 slices bread

1–2 tbsp. mayonnaise   salt and pepper

Recipe #3: _____

½ cup butter   1½ cups flour

1 cup brown sugar   1 tsp. baking soda

2 eggs   ½ tsp. salt

1½ tsp. vanilla   6 oz. chocolate pieces

Recipe #4: _____

1 head lettuce   radishes

1–2 tomatoes   purple onion, sliced

1 cucumber   Italian dressing

READING STRATEGY
Visualizing:
Forming pictures in your mind can help you understand what you are reading.

1. Before You Read It's time for lunch! Talk with a partner. Make a list of three things you both like to eat for lunch.

🎧 **2. Let's Read** Read the recipe for quesadillas. Some words, like *quesadillas*, are not English. As you read, find the words that are borrowed, or that come from, another language; in this case, the words are borrowed from Spanish. Write them down. Then share them with the class.

MEXICAN QUESADILLAS

After trying quesadillas with just cheese, be **adventurous** and **add** some refried beans, guacamole, or black olives

Difficulty: Easy

2 tbsp. shredded cheese, any type

2 flour tortillas

sour cream or salsa
(optional)

Makes 2 servings

quesadilla

1. Place one tortilla on a large plate and sprinkle with the shredded cheese.

2. Top with the second tortilla.

3. Cook in the microwave for about 20-30 seconds until the cheese is melted.

Cool slightly. Use a knife or pizza cutter to cut the tortilla into six wedges. Dip in sour cream or salsa as desired.

The word *until* tells you the time when something stops.

Source: *The Everything® Kids' Cookbook* by Sandra K. Nessenberg

adventurous—willing to try new and different things

add—to put something else in with other things

difficulty—how easy or hard it is to do something

type—a kind

optional—possible, but not necessary

serving—the amount of a food that one person eats

sprinkle—to scatter tiny pieces of something on something else

melted—very hot, soft, and gooey

wedge—a piece of something, shaped like a triangle

3. Unlocking Meaning

❶ **Identifying the Purpose** Choose the sentence that explains the main purpose of the recipe. Check (✓) the correct answer.

_____ 1. to make you want to eat quesadillas

_____ 2. to teach you how to make quesadillas

_____ 3. to teach you words that come from Spanish

❷ **Finding Details** Match each step in the recipe below with the following pictures.

a.

b.

c.

d.

e.

f.

Recipe:

___c___ 1. Place one tortilla on a large plate.

_____ 2. Sprinkle with shredded cheese.

_____ 3. Put the second tortilla on top of the first.

_____ 4. Cook in the microwave until the cheese is melted.

_____ 5. Cool and cut into wedges.

_____ 6. Dip in sour cream and salsa.

❸ **Think about It** Work with a partner. List foods from other countries that people in the U.S. often eat. Tell where each food comes from.

EXAMPLE: *Pizza—Italy*
Burritos—Mexico

❹ **Before You Move On** Work with a partner. Think of a better name for the recipe than "Mexican Quesadillas." Share your ideas with your classmates.

D WORD WORK

1. Word Detective You can often understand the meaning of a compound word by thinking about the meaning of each smaller word:

pan for baking things → baking pan

Match each compound word on the left with its correct meaning on the right.

1. measuring cup   a. a tool you use to slice bread
2. can opener   b. a bowl you use to mix ingredients
3. mixing bowl   c. something you wear on your hand when
4. oven mitt   you take a hot pan out of the oven
5. pizza cutter   d. a tool you use to cut pizzas
6. bread knife   e. a tool you use to open cans
                        f. a cup you use to measure ingredients

2. Word Study The first word in a compound sometimes makes the second word more exact. The first word can come from a *verb* or it can come from a *noun*.

FIRST WORD: VERB	FIRST WORD: NOUN
bowl you use to mix things → mixing bowl	sheet (pan) for making cookie(s) → cookie sheet
cup you use to measure things → measuring cup	tool for peeling vegetable(s) → vegetable peeler

SPELLING AND PHONICS:
To do this activity, go to
page 184.

3. Word Play Work with a partner. Read each of the following definitions. Then write the compound word that goes with each definition. Begin by guessing the compound word, then check your dictionary to check your answers.

1. pan you use to cook sauces (and other liquids)   *saucepan*
2. tool you use to mash potatoes   _____
3. spoons you use to measure things   _____
4. board you cut things on   _____
5. plate you bake pies in   _____
6. tool you use to open bottles   _____

E GRAMMAR   Prepositions That Tell Where

1. Listen Up Listen to each sentence. Point your thumb up 👍 if it sounds correct. Point your thumb down 👎 if it sounds wrong.

👍👎 1. Juan put the ice cream onto the freezer.

👍👎 2. I took the pot off of the stove.

👍👎 3. A sandwich has filling between two slices of bread.

👍👎 4. The pot is on the stove.

👍👎 5. The milk is into the refrigerator.

👍👎 6. Take the milk out of the refrigerator.

2. Learn the Rule Prepositions often tell us where something is. Learn how "place" prepositions are used by reading the following rules. Then do Activity 1 again.

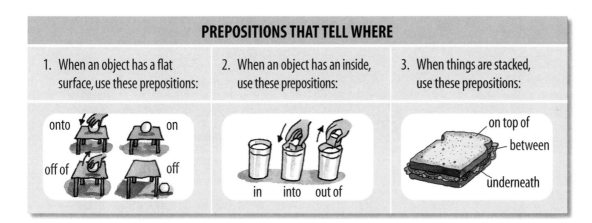

PREPOSITIONS THAT TELL WHERE

1. When an object has a flat surface, use these prepositions:
   onto on off of off

2. When an object has an inside, use these prepositions:
   in into out of

3. When things are stacked, use these prepositions:
   on top of between underneath

3. Practice the Rule Work with a partner. Write a sentence for each preposition about things in your classroom.

1. (on) _____
2. (onto) _____
3. (on top of) _____
4. (off) _____
5. (off of) _____
6. (out of) _____
7. (in) _____
8. (into) _____
9. (underneath) _____
10. (between) _____

F **BRIDGE TO WRITING** Recipes

1. Before You Read Look at the recipe below. What is for dinner?

2. Let's Read Read the following recipe for meatloaf. **Visualize**, or form pictures in your mind, of the steps in the recipe as you read.

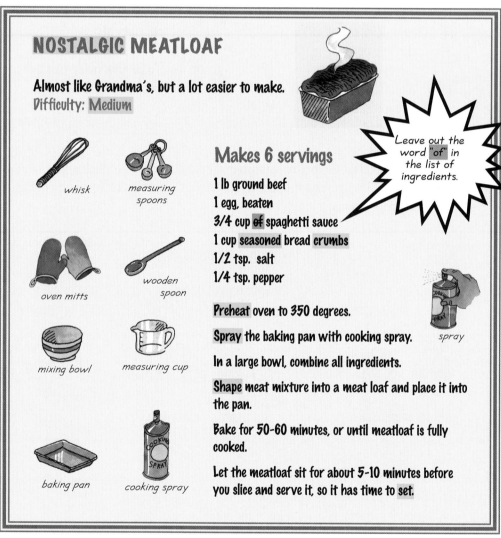

NOSTALGIC MEATLOAF

Almost like Grandma's, but a lot easier to make.
Difficulty: Medium

whisk

measuring spoons

oven mitts

wooden spoon

mixing bowl

measuring cup

baking pan

cooking spray

spray

Leave out the word "of" in the list of ingredients.

Makes 6 servings

1 lb ground beef
1 egg, beaten
3/4 cup of spaghetti sauce
1 cup seasoned bread crumbs
1/2 tsp. salt
1/4 tsp. pepper

Preheat oven to 350 degrees.

Spray the baking pan with cooking spray.

In a large bowl, combine all ingredients.

Shape meat mixture into a meat loaf and place it into the pan.

Bake for 50-60 minutes, or until meatloaf is fully cooked.

Let the meatloaf sit for about 5-10 minutes before you slice and serve it, so it has time to **set**.

Source: *The Everything® Kid's Cookbook* by Sandra K Nessnberg

nostalgic—making you remember happy past times

medium—in between; moderate

seasoned—having flavor from herbs, spices, or salt

crumb—a very small piece of bread or cake

preheat—to heat an oven to a certain temperature before putting food in it

spray—to put a liquid onto something using a pressurized can

shape—to form something with your hands

set—to become solid

3. Making Content Connections Talk with a partner. Do you know how to cook? Think of one dish for each meal or snack that you can make *without* using a recipe. Then complete the chart below.

Meal	You	Your Partner
breakfast		
lunch		
snack		
dinner		

4. Expanding Your Vocabulary When people talk, they often use expressions, or groups of words, with a special meaning. Work with a partner. First, match each of the following highlighted food words or phrases with its definition below. Then write a sentence using each expression.

a.

The test was a piece of cake. It wasn't difficult at all.

b.

I live in the Big Apple. I love this city!

c.

Don't be chicken! It's not dangerous.

d.

Mary spilled the beans. She told Tommy that I like him.

e.

Juan had to eat his words when he realized he wasn't right.

f.

That's baloney! I don't believe you.

___c___ 1. afraid

_____ 2. something silly or not true

_____ 3. very easy

_____ 4. to admit being wrong

_____ 5. to tell a secret

_____ 6. a nickname for New York City

G WRITING CLINIC — Recipes

1. Think about It Where are three places you often find recipes?

2. Focus on Organization

❶ Read the following recipe and the description of each part of the recipe.

S'more is short for "some more." "I'll have some more!"

Every recipe has a name

Recipes often have a short introduction.

Sometimes a recipe tells you if the recipe is easy or hard.

This tells how much or how many the recipe will make.

The recipe lists the ingredients—and tells how much or how many

Here are the utensils you will need

The steps are listed in time order.

Recipes sometimes have an ending that tells you what the dish goes with.

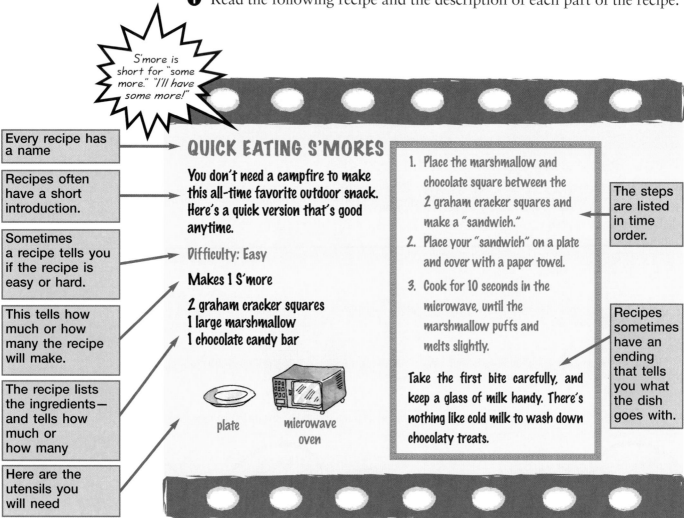

QUICK EATING S'MORES

You don't need a campfire to make this all-time favorite outdoor snack. Here's a quick version that's good anytime.

Difficulty: Easy

Makes 1 S'more

2 graham cracker squares
1 large marshmallow
1 chocolate candy bar

plate   microwave oven

1. Place the marshmallow and chocolate square between the 2 graham cracker squares and make a "sandwich."
2. Place your "sandwich" on a plate and cover with a paper towel.
3. Cook for 10 seconds in the microwave, until the marshmallow puffs and melts slightly.

Take the first bite carefully, and keep a glass of milk handy. There's nothing like cold milk to wash down chocolaty treats.

Source: *The Everything® Kids' Cookbook* by Sandra K. Nessenberg

❷ Imagine that you are writing a recipe for making hard-boiled eggs. Number the steps below so that they are in the correct time order from step 1 to step 5.

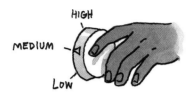

_____ a. When the water boils, turn the heat to medium and let the water simmer (cook slowly) for 12–15 minutes.

_____ b. Gently crack the eggshells and peel them off.

_____ c. Put the saucepan over high heat and bring the water to a boil.

___1___ d. Put the eggs in a small saucepan, and fill the pan with enough water to cover the eggs.

_____ e. Take the saucepan off the heat and pour cold water into the pan to cool the eggs. Cool the eggs for several minutes.

3. Focus on Style Recipes often have interesting names that make them sound delicious. Match the description of each dish on the left with its correct name on the right.

1. Dish with beans and beef you eat in a bowl
2. Sandwich with melted cheese and tuna, served hot
3. Round and golden, you eat them for breakfast with syrup
4. Dish with beans, rice, and meat wrapped in a tortilla
5. Soup you love on a cold day
6. Dish you often serve with chicken or other meat at dinner
7. Fruit-flavored party drink

a. Super Burrito Grande
b. Old Fashioned Mashed Potatoes
c. Texas Chili
d. Tropical Punch
e. Fluffy Buttermilk Pancakes
f. Tasty Tuna Melt
g. Creamy Clam Chowder

H WRITER'S WORKSHOP   Recipes

Create a class cookbook. Contribute your favorite recipe. *Important*:
Write your own recipe. Do not copy the recipe from another cookbook.

1. Getting It Out

❶ Decide what you will make. Make a list of dishes you like. Here are
some possibilities.

1.

pancakes, muffins,
scrambled eggs

Breakfast

2.

sandwich, burrito, salad

Lunch

3.

tacos   *fried rice*   *spaghetti*

Dinner

4.

nachos, guacamole dip, lumpia

Appetizers

5.

trail mix, cookies, popcorn

Snacks

6.

cake, banana split, pie

Desserts

❷ Choose two or three dishes on your list. Then, to help decide which
dish you will teach others to make, ask yourself a few questions:

1. Is this a dish others might like to make?
2. Do I already know how to make this dish? Is there someone in my
   family that can show me how to make the dish?
3. Is it easy to explain in words how to make this dish?

❸ Here is how Juan answered these questions. Which dish do you think Juan should choose?

Possible Recipes	Is this a dish others would like to make?	Do I know how to make this?	How easy is it to explain how to make this?
Hard-boiled egg	Probably not.	Yes	Very easy
Chocolate peanut butter pudding	YES!!!	Dad knows how to make this. He can help me.	Probably easy.
Fried rice	Not sure.	No. (We always get take out.)	Hard. Lots of ingredients.

❹ Learn how to make the dish you have chosen from your list of recipes. Get help from an adult. Ask questions and take notes. Read Juan's notes below.

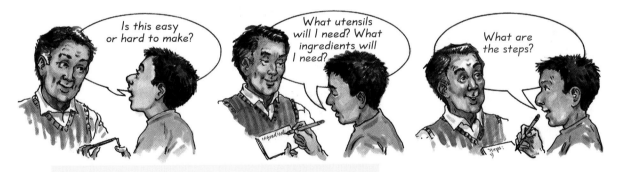

Chocolate Peanut Butter Pudding

—Really easy to make

—Need large bowl, measuring cup, whisk, spatula, saucepan

—Ingredients: 1 package of instant chocolate pudding

MINI-LESSON
Use numbers to show time order:
1. Prepare...

2. Getting It Down

❶ Turn your notes into an outline. Complete the outline below.

Recipe for: _____

Difficulty: _____

Servings: _____

Utensils needed:

_____   _____

_____   _____

Ingredients needed:

_____   _____

_____   _____

_____   _____

Directions:

1. _____
2. _____
3. _____
4. _____

❷ Now, turn your outline into a recipe. Here is the recipe Juan wrote. What do you think? Do you want to make Chunky Chocolate Peanut Butter Pudding?

Juan's recipe has a cute name. He begins with a sentence that makes you hungry. He tells you the recipe is easy to make.

Juan lists the utensils you will need.

Juan lists the ingredients. He tells you how many and how much. He tells how many servings the recipe will make.

The steps are in time order. They are easy to understand.

Chunky Chocolate Peanut Butter Pudding

This is so good you'll eat the whole thing!

Difficulty: Easy

Makes 4 servings

Utensils: bowl, measuring cup, wire whisk, spatula, saucepan

1 package instant chocolate pudding $\frac{1}{2}$ cup peanut butter

2 cups cold milk $\frac{1}{4}$ cup chopped nuts (optional)

1. Prepare the pudding. Follow the directions on the package.
2. Use the whisk to stir the peanut butter into the pudding.
3. Pour the pudding into serving dishes.
4. Sprinkle with chopped nuts.

Refrigerate until ready to serve.

3. Getting It Right Take a careful look at what you have written.
Use this guide to help you revise your recipe.

Question to Ask	How to Check	How to Revise
1. Does my recipe have a name and short introduction?	Circle the name and underline the introduction.	Add a cute name or write a sentence that makes the cook want to make your recipe.
2. Did I list the utensils and ingredients? Did I tell how much or how many?	Put a check mark (✓) next to each utensil, ingredient, and amount.	Add utensils, ingredients, and the amount next to each ingredient.
3. Did I remember each step? Are the steps in time order?	Pretend that you are following the recipe. Act out each step in your head.	Add a step or change the order.

4. Presenting It

❶ Share your recipe with your classmates.

❷ Ask for volunteers to repeat each step in your recipe, using their own words.

❸ As you listen to others, take notes. Use a note-taking guide like this one.

```
Utensils:                           Ingredients:
1. _____          _____
2. _____          _____
3. _____          _____

Steps:
1. _____
2. _____
3. _____
```

1. On Assignment Does your school have a classroom with kitchen appliances? Choose a volunteer "head chef" to show your class how to make a dish.

❶ Before you begin, listen as your teacher helps the class understand basic safety and kitchen rules.

❷ Listen as the chef reads the recipe aloud. Which utensils will he or she need? What are the ingredients?

❸ Watch carefully as the chef shows how to prepare the dish. Clap quietly, but do not talk or interrupt.

❹ Who will set the table? Look at the picture. What do you think is missing?

Safety and Kitchen Rules

Wash your hands before touching food.
Start with a clean cooking area.
Learn how to use each appliance.
Be careful with knives.
Be careful using electric or gas appliances.
Always use potholders or oven mitts.
Keep the cooking area clean as you work.

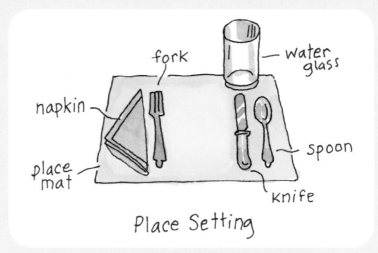

Place Setting

❺ Time to eat! Ask the chef if you may taste the dish.

❻ Compliment the chef. Say something nice about the dish.

It's delicious!

Very tasty!

My compliments to the chef!

2. Link to Literature

🎧 **SHARED READING** Read the following recipe poem. The poet is unknown.

LET'S TALK Answer the following questions.

1. Look again at the verbs in the poem. Why is this called a "recipe poem"?

2. What is the "large blue bowl" in the first line?

3. Can you think of one more thing you might "mix" into the weather poem?

JUST FOR FUN Write a recipe poem of your own with four lines.

1. Choose a topic. Use one of these of think of your own.

_____ school

_____ friends

_____ learning English

2. Begin each line with a cooking verb.

Take _____

Add _____

Stir in _____

Mix _____

A Recipe for Weather

Begin with a large blue bowl

Take a sprinkle of yellow sun

Cover it with dark clouds

Add swirling winds

Pour falling rain

Stir in loud crashing thunder

Mix together with a feather

And you've made a day of weather.

Source: humanitiessoftware.com

swirling—going around and around

crashing—making a sudden noise

feather—one of the light, soft things that cover a bird

The Top Five

Read...

■ Survey reports about what people like most, from *TIME For Kids* magazine. Kids share their favorite things with researchers.

Link to Literature

■ A list poem written by a student.

Objectives:

Reading:
■ A report: Understanding an information survey
■ Strategies: Comparing information, noting surprising facts
■ Literature: Reading a list poem

Writing:
■ Writing a short research report that involves a survey
■ Listing information in order
■ Making a chart that presents data

Vocabulary:
■ Recognizing word families: Nouns and verbs that are the same word
■ Learning math vocabulary

Listening/Speaking:
■ Listening for information
■ Interviewing others (to take a survey)
■ Giving a short oral report

Grammar:
■ Forming present tense questions

Spelling and Phonics:
■ Learning about digraphs

BEFORE YOU BEGIN

Talk with your classmates.

1. Look at the picture. Read what each student says. What do you think the woman is asking?
2. Who could the woman be? What could her job be?
3. Imagine that you are in the picture. How would you answer the question?

A CONNECTING TO YOUR LIFE

1. Tuning In Listen to a woman interview a group of students. What are the students telling us?

☐ They are telling us what they like best for dinner.

☐ They are telling us their favorite pizza toppings.

☐ They are telling us how to make a good pizza.

2. Talking It Over

Imagine that your class is visiting a non-fat frozen yogurt factory. Order your favorite flavor! Which flavor is at the top of your class list?

1.

vanilla

2.

chocolate

3.

strawberry

4.

neopolitan

5.

butter pecan

6.

black cherry

7.

pepper-mint

8.

chocolate chip

9.

rocky road

Read the title of this unit. What do you think the unit is probably about? Check (✓) the correct answer.

_____ 1. It's about things people like best or most.

_____ 2. It's about frozen yogurt toppings.

_____ 3. It's about things that cost less than five dollars.

B GETTING READY TO READ

1. Learning New Words Read the sentences below. Try to figure out the meanings of the underlined words.

1. Maria likes basketball better than other sports. Maria <u>prefers</u> basketball to other sports.
2. Out of 100 kids, 50 like vanilla frozen yogurt best. That's 50 <u>percent</u>.
3. <u>According to</u> the TV weather report, it will be sunny tomorrow.
4. California is the most popular state to visit—it's <u>number one</u>!
5. Tran is asking kids what kind of fruit they like best. He is taking a <u>survey</u> about fruit.
6. I read in The New York Times that Graciela Pérez will run for president. The New York Times is the <u>source</u> of that story.

Now match the word or phrase on the left with its correct definition on the right.

1. prefer   a. the best or most important person or thing
2. percent (%)   b. to like something better than something else
3. according to   c. a person or book you get information from
4. number one   d. said or written by someone
5. survey   e. the amount in every hundred
6. source   f. a set of questions you ask other people to find out what they like or think

2. Talking It Over Work in a group. Look Have everyone in the group pick their five favorite frozen yogurt flavors, then rank them below (the flavor with the most votes is number one, etc.).

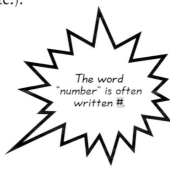

_____ Our #1 choice

_____ Our #2 choice

_____ Our #3 choice

_____ Our #4 choice

_____ Our #5 choice

The word "number" is often written #.

C READING TO LEARN   Surveys

1. Before You Read Imagine a really hot summer day. What would most people eat or drink to stay cool? Share your ideas with a partner.

2. Let's Read Read each of the following surveys. **Compare** the results of the first survey with your own "top five" list.

Top Five Favorite Frozen Yogurt Flavors

When the temperature rises, frozen yogurt can really beat the heat. Check out the coolest flavors in America:

1. Vanilla 28%
2. Chocolate 8%
3. Neapolitan 7% (vanilla, chocolate, strawberry)
4. Butter pecan 4.5%
5. Chocolate chip 3.5%

> The word *cool* can mean *low in temperature* or it can mean that you *really like something.*

> 4.5% is pronounced "four point five percent."

Top Five Healthy Beverages

According to 2,400 kids in the U.S., Germany, France, China, Japan, and Britain, orange juice is number one. But milk is a close second in the U.S. Here are American kids' favorite healthy drinks:

Orange juice 29%
Milk 28%
Energy drinks 22%
Apple juice 22%
Water 23%

temperature—how hot or cold something is

beat the heat—to stay cool when the weather is hot

beverage—something to drink

close second—a person or thing that is almost in first place

3. Unlocking Meaning

❶ **Finding the Main Idea** Each of the surveys above answers a question. What questions does each survey answer? Check (✓) the correct answers.

1. Top Five Flavors of Non-Fat Frozen Yogurt

_____ a. Why do many people like frozen yogurt?

_____ b. What are the flavors of frozen yogurt people like most?

_____ c. How do you make frozen yogurt?

2. Top Five Healthy Beverages

_____ a. Do American kids drink too many soft drinks?

_____ b. Which companies sell orange juice?

_____ c. What healthy drinks do kids like best?

❷ **Finding Details** Read each of the following sentences. Write _T_ for True and _F_ for False.

_____ 1. Many people like to eat ice cream on hot days.

_____ 2. Vanilla is everyone's favorite frozen yogurt.

_____ 3. Chocolate frozen yogurt is a close second to vanilla in the U.S.

_____ 4. More people like chocolate chip than butter pecan.

_____ 5. Orange juice is the favorite drink of kids around the world.

_____ 6. Milk is the second favorite drink of kids around the world.

_____ 7. American kids like orange juice better than milk.

❸ **Think about It** Look again at the first survey. The percentages add up to _less than 100%_. Choose the best reason for this. Check (✔) the correct answer.

_____ 1. A lot of people named other flavors.

_____ 2. The report is wrong.

_____ 3. The number 4.5% is wrong. It should be 45%.

Now look at the second survey. The percentages add up to _more than 100%_. Choose the best reason for this. Check (✔) the correct answer.

_____ 1. A lot of people can't tell the difference between orange juice and apple juice.

_____ 2. Many people probably named more than one favorite drink.

_____ 3. Water should not be on the list.

❹ **Before You Move On** Work with a partner. Make an ad for your favorite drink. Share your ad with classmates.

D WORD WORK

1. Word Detective The same word in a word family can have two different jobs. Read the sentences below. Write *N* if the underlined word in the sentence is a noun. Write *V* if the word is a verb.

<u> N </u>   1. Many people dislike the desert. They hate the <u>heat</u>.

_____   2. I'm hungry! Let's <u>heat</u> the oven and bake a pizza!

_____   3. My favorite <u>drink</u> is milk.

_____   4. I love to <u>drink</u> milk.

_____   5. Juan's favorite drink is <u>milk</u>, too.

_____   6. Do you know how to <u>milk</u> a cow?

_____   7. That was a good <u>guess</u>!

_____   8. Try to <u>guess</u> the answer.

2. Word Study Two (or more) words belong to the same "word family" when they have related meanings, but have different jobs in a sentence.

Nouns	Verbs
Ms. Yee always gives me good <u>grades</u>.	Ms. Yee <u>grades</u> hard. She hardly ever gives A's.
Ms. Yee lets us work in small <u>groups</u>.	Ms. Yee often <u>groups</u> the seventh graders together.

SPELLING AND PHONICS:
To do this activity, go to page 185. ■ ■ ■

3. Word Play The underlined words below are *verbs*. Complete the second sentences with *nouns*.

1. Juan always <u>salts</u> his food. Too much ___*salt*___ isn't good for him.

2. Margaret always <u>laughs</u> at my jokes. She has a funny _____.

3. Please <u>slice</u> the pie in eight pieces. Give each person a _____.

4. Does your sandwich <u>taste</u> OK? My sandwich has a funny _____.

5. Tran likes to <u>cook</u>. He wants to be a _____ when he grows up.

6. Juana <u>painted</u> her bedroom walls purple. She put green _____ on the ceiling!

E GRAMMAR — Present Tense Questions

1. Listen Up Listen to the conversation. Hold up one finger ☝ if the sentence is a question. Hold up two fingers ✌ if the sentence is an answer.

  1. Who is your favorite teacher?

  3. Who's your favorite teacher, Tran?

2. I like Ms. Vasquez.

4. I like Mr. Gold...and Ms. Lee.

2. Learn the Rule There are a few different ways to form a question. Read the following rules. Then do Activity 1 again.

PRESENT TENSE QUESTIONS				
	Question Word	Helping Verb	Subject	Main Verb + Rest of Sentence
When the answer to your question is *yes* or *no*, begin your question with **do** or **does**.		*Do* *Does*	*you/we/they he/she/it*	*like ice cream?*
When you are asking for information about a thing, use **what**.	*What*	*do*	*you*	*like to do after school?*
When you are asking about a person, use **who**.	*Who*	*does*	*Juan*	*like best?*
When you are asking about several different choices, you often use **which**.	*Which*	*do*	*you*	*like best— dogs or cats?*

3. Practice the Rule Work with a partner. Write a question for each of the answers below. Practice asking and answering the questions.

_____   1. I eat burritos for lunch.

_____   2. I prefer milk.

_____   3. I like PE best.

_____   4. I hang out with Stefan.

_____   5. I like to watch TV.

_____   6. I like fruit for dessert.

F BRIDGE TO WRITING   Surveys

1. Before You Read What is your favorite subject in school? Share the information with a partner.

2. Let's Read As you read, take notes on a separate piece of paper about any facts that surprise you. Be ready to share them later.

Top Five Favorite Subjects

Can you guess which school subjects kids like the best? (Recess doesn't count.) Researchers asked 1,016 students ages 10 to 17 this question. More than 1 in 4 picked math. Here are subjects that make the grade.

- 28% Math
- 21% Science
- 16% Art
- 15% History/Social Studies
- 13% English

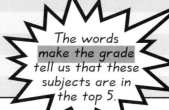

The words make the grade tell us that these subjects are in the top 5.

Top Five Favorite Kids Books of All Time

What's the best book you have ever read? That's the question the National Education Association asked in a recent survey of 1,800 students ages 7 to 15. Here are their top picks:

1. Harry Potter (series)–J.K.Rowling
2. Goosebumps (series)–R.L. Stine
3. Green Eggs and Ham–Dr. Seuss
4. The Cat in the Hat–Dr. Seuss
5. Arthur (series)–Marc Brown

  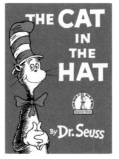 

HARRY POTTER and all related characters and elements are trademarks of and © Warner Bros. Entertainment Inc.

recess—free time during the school day

researcher—someone who studies a subject

pick—the best thing out of a group

series—a set of things, like books, that come one after another

3. Making Content Connections Work with a partner. Discuss your favorites for each of the following groups. Then complete the chart below.

What is your favorite...	You	Your partner
...ice cream flavor? Why?		
...drink? Why?		
...school subject? Why?		
...book? Why?		

4. Expanding Your Vocabulary Surveys often include numbers, such as fractions (½), decimals (.50), and percentages (50%). Complete the chart below with the numbers from the box. Write the numbers that mean the same thing. Practice saying the numbers aloud.

~~.50~~	¾	33%	¹⁄₁₀	⅔	25%
67%	.10	~~50%~~	.33	¼	.75

Fraction	1/2			1/3		
Decimal	.50	.25			.67	
Percent	50%		75%			10%

Sources: "Top Five Favorite Subjects," *TIME For Kids*, Nov. 26, 1997, Vol. 3, No. 9, p. 2. Used with permission from TIME For Kids Magazine.
"Top Five Favorite Kids' Books of All Time," *TIME For Kids*, Sept. 12, 2003, Vol. 9, No. 11, p. 3. Used with permission from TIME For Kids Magazine.

G WRITING CLINIC   Surveys

1. Think about It A survey is a type of report. What does a report usually tell you?

☐ facts you didn't know   ☐ how to make something   ☐ a story that is true

2. Focus on Organization

❶ Look again at the survey report on kids' favorite books.

Top Five Favorite Kids Books of All Time

What's the best book you have ever read? That's the question the National Education Association asked in a recent survey of 1,800 students ages 7 to 15. Here are their top picks:

1. **Harry Potter (series)–J.K.Rowling**
2. **Goosebumps (series)–R.L. Stine**
3. **Green Eggs and Ham–Dr. Seuss**
4. **The Cat in the Hat–Dr. Seuss**
5. **Arthur (series)–Marc Brown**

The title tells you what the survey report is about

A survey often has an introduction. It often states the question the survey asked. The introduction explains who was asked the question.

The results, or answers, are often in a list.

The survey names the source of the information.

Source: "Top Five Favorite Kids' Books of All Time," *TIME For Kids*, Sept. 12, 2003, Vol. 9, No. 11, p. 3. Used with permission from *TIME For Kids Magazine*.

HARRY POTTER and all related characters and elements are trademarks of and © Warner Bros. Entertainment Inc.

❷ Now read the survey about school subjects one more time.

Top Five Favorite Subjects

[1] Can you guess which school subjects kids like the best? (Recess doesn't count.) [2] Researchers asked 1,016 students ages 10 to 17 this question. [3] More than 1 in 4 picked math. [4] Here are subjects that make the grade.

28% Math
21% Science
16% Art
15% History/Social Studies
13% English

❸ Answer the following questions.

1. Which sentence asks the survey question? Sentence #_____

2. Which sentence tells who was asked the survey question? Sentence #_____

3. Which sentence tells you about the results of the survey? Sentence #_____

❹ What is missing from this survey? Check (✓) the correct answer.

_____ title   _____ introduction   _____ source

3. Focus on Style
Every report needs an introduction. Read both of these introductions.

a. We asked 2,400 kids around the world to name their favorite beverage. Here is what they told us:

b. What do kids prefer to drink when they are thirsty? We asked 2,400 kids around the world to name their favorite beverage. Here is what they told us:

❶ What is the difference between the two introductions? Which one is more interesting? Why?

❷ Asking a question is a good way to begin an introduction. Match each survey title on the left with an introductory question on the right.

1. Top 5 Film Actors
2. Top 5 Most Popular Desserts
3. Top 5 Kinds of Music
4. Top 5 School Subjects
5. Top 5 After-school Activities

a. What do kids like to do when school is over?
b. What classes do American students enjoy most?
c. Who are Americans' favorite stars?
d. What do music fans listen to on the radio?
e. How do Americans like to end a meal?

H WRITER'S WORKSHOP

Surveys

What do other kids like? Find out for yourself and tell others! Write your own survey report.

1. Getting It Out

❶ What do you want to learn? Look at the following survey ideas, or think of your own.

a.

Favorite TV shows

b.

Favorite music

c.

Favorite desserts

d.

Favorite pets

e.

Favorite sports

f.

You decide!

❷ Write the question you will ask.

EXAMPLE: *What is your favorite after-school activity?*

QUESTION: _____

❸ Decide who you will interview, or talk to. Plan to interview 10 people or more.

Your classmates

Kids in other classes

Family members and neighbors

❹ Conduct your interview. Write down each person's answer in a notebook while you are talking to them.

What is your favorite after-school activity?

Play sports

Play basketball

Hang out with my friends

Go over to my best friend's house

Be with my friends

Get a pizza

Watch TV

Play soccer

Go to the sandwich shop

Do homework

Watch TV

Play volleyball

Play football

❺ Organize and tally, or count, the results.

Play sports (5 kids)

Do things with friends (3 kids)

Go get something to eat (2 kids)

Watch TV (2 kids)

Do homework (1 kid)

> **MINI-LESSON**
> When you make a list that is in order of importance, number each item starting with "1."

2. Getting It Down

❶ Make an outline to help you organize your survey results. Use a planner like the one below.

TITLE: Top Five _____.

- -

INTRODUCTION

My question: _____?

Who I talked to: _____.

- -

RESULTS

Here are the _____ that kids like most:

1. _____ _____%
2. _____ _____%
3. _____ _____%
4. _____ _____%
5. _____ _____%

Figure out percentages if you interviewed a lot of kids.

SOURCE (Your name): _____

---

❷ Now, turn your outline into a report on the survey you took. Here is what Graciela wrote in her survey. What do you think?

Graciela states the question in her introduction. She tells us how many kids she interviewed.

Top 5 After School Activities

What do kids like to do best after school? I asked 13 classmates. Here is what they said:

1. Play sports   38%
2. Do things with friends   23%
3. Go get something to eat   15%
4. Watch TV   15%
5. Do homework   8%

She lists the results in order.

Source: Graciela Alvarez, Kennedy Middle School

---

❸ Write a list of your results on a large piece of paper to use when you present your report.

3. Getting It Right

Take a careful look at your report. Use this guide to make it better.

Question to Ask	How to Check	How to Revise
1. Does my report have a good introduction?	Circle the question that your survey answers. Underline the sentence that explains who you interviewed.	Begin your introduction with a question. Be specific. Explain who you interviewed, how many people there were, and how old they were.
2. Did I present the results accurately and clearly?	Check to see that the order of the items is correct.	Change the order if you need to.
3. Did I state the source?	Put a star (★) next to the source.	Add your own name as the source of the survey.

4. Presenting It Read your report to your classmates.

❶ Begin by reading the title.

❷ Next, read the introduction. Read slowly and speak clearly.

❸ Show your classmates the list with your results. Read the list.

1) Play sports
2) Do things with friends
3) Get something to eat
4) Watch TV
5) Do homework

❹ Ask for feedback.

You chose an interesting question to ask.

You talked to lots of kids.

Your chart is easy to read.

1. On Assignment Make a pie chart that shows your survey results.

❶ Gather your materials. These are the things you will need.

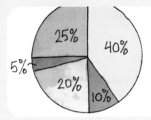

- Large sheet of paper
- Pencil
- Black pen
- Colored markers
- Protractor
- Compass (or coffee can lid)

❷ Draw a circle on the sheet of paper. Use a compass, coffee can lid, or other round object as a guide. Use pencil to draw the circle.

❸ Turn each percentage on your chart into a decimal.

50% = .50	
25% = .25	

vanilla	.50 X 360° = 180°
chocolate	.25 X 360° = 90°
strawberry	.10 X 360° = 36°

❹ Next, change the decimals into degrees. To do this, multiply each decimal figure by 360° (degrees).

❺ Use your protractor to measure each piece of the pie.

❻ Color each section of the pie a different color.

❼ Label each section of your pie chart.

❽ Share your pie chart and the results of your survey with your classmates.

2. Link to Literature

SHARED READING Read this list poem written by a student.

LET'S TALK Answer the following questions.

1. Why is this kind of poem called a "list poem"?
2. What is the poem about?
3. Suppose you wanted to write a list poem about your "top five" favorites. What would you write about?

JUST FOR FUN Write your own "top five" list poem.

My locker has

dirty gym socks

last week's assignments

crumpled papers

broken pencils

dirty Kleenex

saxophone reeds

apple cores

rotten banana peels

overdue library books

and a lock that will not open.

Source: *Love Me When I'm Most Unlovable*
by Robert Ricken

assignment—a piece of schoolwork

crumpled—crushed into a ball

broken—cracked in pieces

reed—a thin piece of wood attached to the mouthpiece of an instrument to help it make a sound

core—the center of something, like an apple

rotten—going bad or decaying

overdue—late being returned to the library

Memories

Read...

- Selections from "My First Sports Memory," from *Sports Illustrated for Kids*. Learn about star athletes and the highlights of their early, early, early careers!

Link to Literature

- A memory poem written by a student.

Objectives:

Reading:
- Responding to personal memories
- Strategy: Questioning the author
- Literature: Reading a memory poem

Writing:
- Writing a personal memory
- Expressing feelings
- Using adjectives to express emotion

Vocabulary:
- Recognizing synonyms
- Learning sports vocabulary

Listening/Speaking:
- Listening to a short narrative
- Presenting a personal memory to others
- Speaking with expression

Grammar:
- Understanding the simple past tense

Spelling and Phonics:
- Pronouncing words with silent consonants

Ramon Cisneros,
when he hit his first home run

BEFORE YOU BEGIN

Talk with your classmates.

1. Look at the picture. What is the boy doing?
2. Read the caption. What is the boy's name?
3. What story does the picture tell? Help your teacher write several sentences about the picture.

A CONNECTING TO YOUR LIFE

1. Tuning In Listen to an interview with Bernie Davis, a star player for the New York Yankees. He started playing Little League baseball when he was young. What does he remember about that experience?

☐ He broke his bat.　　☐ He won the game for his team.　　☐ He learned he could run fast.

2. Talking It Over

Talk with a partner. Share one or more of your own childhood memories and the feelings that you remember from that time.

Something that...

...*made me happy*

...*made me excited*

...*made me mad*

...*made me sad*

Read the title of this unit. What do you think the unit is probably about? Check (✓) the correct answer.

_____ 1. It's about how to teach children.

_____ 2. It's about memories from childhood.

_____ 3. It's about how to play sports.

B GETTING READY TO READ

1. Learning New Words Read the sentences below. Try to figure out the meanings of the underlined words.

1. Juan screams when he sees a spider. He is <u>afraid of</u> spiders.
2. We watched the <u>All-Star</u> Game on TV. Both teams had their best players.
3. The New York Yankees play in the American League. The Los Angeles Dodgers play in the National League. The two teams play in different baseball <u>leagues</u>.
4. Pele is still the world's most famous soccer player. He is a <u>legend</u>.
5. Ben didn't expect a call from Jennifer. He was <u>surprised</u> to hear her voice.
6. Our team scored more points than the other team. We <u>won</u> the game!
7. The other team <u>lost</u> the game. They scored fewer points than we did.

Match each word on the left with the correct definition on the right.

1. afraid of
2. all-star
3. league
4. legend
5. surprise
6. win
7. lose

a. a feeling you have when something happens that you don't expect
b. to be first in a game or contest
c. frightened by something
d. involving only the top athletes
e. to come in last in a game or contest
f. a group of sports teams that play against each other
g. someone who is famous for being very good at something

> An experience is something that happens to you in life.

2. Talking It Over Work in a small group. Talk about an experience from your life that you will never forget. Share your feelings about it. Look at the following examples for ideas.

A time you learned to do something

Something you did for the first time

Something you did with your family or friends

A special event you remember

Memories 131

C **READING TO LEARN**   **Personal Memories**

1. Before You Read Look at the pictures and the source information below. Who do you think these people are?

☐ athletes   ☐ actors   ☐ students like you

 2. Let's Read A magazine asked some star athletes about their early sports memories. As you read, think of a question you would like to ask one of them.

I skied and tore ligaments in my knee when I was five. The next day, my brother tore his ligaments! We sledded the rest of the winter.
—**Jonny Moseley**, skier
Hometown: San Francisco, California

The first time I had a chance to carry the football as a running back was when I was seven years old. I scored five touchdowns in one game!
—**Terrell Davis**, running back, Denver Broncos
Hometown: San Diego, California

I was the first girl to play in the all-boys' summer basketball league. I ended up doing really well. Everybody was surprised, and it was a lot of fun.
—**Nykesha Sales**, guard, Orlando Miracle
Hometown: Bloomfield, Connecticut

Source: *Sports Illustrated for Kids*

---

tore—the past tense of the verb *tear*, which means to rip or split apart

ligament—one of the "bands" that hold your bones together

sled—to ride a vehicle that slides over snow

touchdown—the action of moving the football into the other team's end zone to score points

3. Unlocking Meaning

❶ Finding the Main Idea Choose the best ending for each of the following statements. Check (✓) the correct answer.

1. Jonny Moseley remembers the time...

_____ a. ...he fell down in the snow.

_____ b. ...he hurt his knee while he was skiing.

_____ c. ...he learned to ride a sled.

2. Terrell Davis remembers the time...

_____ a. ...he played quarterback on his team.

_____ b. ...he scored the most touchdowns in one season.

_____ c. ...he scored a lot of touchdowns in a single game.

3. Nykesha Sales remembers the time...

_____ a. ...she played in an all-boys' basketball league.

_____ b. ...she was the best player in the league.

_____ c. ...she learned how to play basketball.

❷ Finding Details Read the sentences below. Write *T* for True or *F* for False.

_____ 1. Jonny hurt his knee while he was skiing.

_____ 2. Jonny's knee got better in a couple of days.

_____ 3. Terrell Davis grew up in San Diego, California.

_____ 4. Terrell was the star quarterback in the league.

_____ 5. Many people were amazed that Nykesha was so good at basketball.

_____ 6. Nykesha played basketball better than many of the boys.

❸ Think about It Reread Nykesha's sports memory. Which of the following sentences explains how she felt about her experience?

1. She felt proud because she played so well.
2. She felt foolish playing on a boys' team.
3. She felt jealous of the boys because they played better.

❹ Before You Move On Talk with a partner. Which sports memory was most interesting to read? Why?

D WORD WORK

1. Word Detective All these adjectives explain how people feel. Match each word on the left with the word on the right that means the same thing (or almost the same thing).

happy

1. surprised   a. frightened
2. great   b. shocked
3. sad   c. angry
4. happy   d. glad
5. afraid   e. unhappy
6. mad   f. wonderful

2. Word Study Two words that mean almost the same thing are called synonyms. Knowing synonyms can help you choose just the right word for a sentence.

fun   Baseball is <u>fun</u>.
enjoyable   Monday Night Football is <u>enjoyable</u>.

3. Word Play Work with a partner. Rewrite each of the sentences below. Replace each underlined word with a word from the box. You can use your dictionary.

| ~~furious~~ | terrific | cheerful |
| scared | alone | terrible |

1. My father was <u>mad</u>.
   My father was furious.

2. Juan feels <u>lonely</u>.
   _____

3. We had a <u>great</u> time at the game.
   _____

4. Michele is <u>afraid</u> of dogs.
   _____

5. Maria is a <u>happy</u> person.
   _____

6. Tran is sick. He feels <u>very bad</u>.
   _____

SPELLING AND PHONICS:
To do this activity, go to page 185.

E GRAMMAR — Simple Past Tense

1. Listen Up You usually use the simple past tense to talk about the past. Listen to each sentence. Point your thumb up 👍 if it sounds correct, or down 👎 if it sounds wrong.

1. When I was ten, I played softball.
2. Jonny fall and hurted his knee.
3. We sledded over the snow.
4. The game yesterday is a lot of fun.
5. The team losed every game.
6. I was a ball boy for the Yankees when I was young.

2. Learn the Rule Use the past tense to talk about things that happened to you in the past. Learn about the past tense by reading the rules below. Then do Activity 1 again.

THE SIMPLE PAST TENSE

Use the past tense to describe an action or event that took place at a specific time in the past.

1. *Regular* verbs add **–ed** or sometimes just **–d** to form the past tense.

   *Ken plays baseball. When he was ten, he play**ed** on a Little League team.*

2. *Irregular* verbs have past tense forms that can be very different from the present tense. Check the Irregular Verbs List on page 200 in your book if you're not sure.

   *Tony's soccer team usually wins. Last year, the team **won** every game!*

3. Practice the Rule Work with a partner. Write the past tense form of each verb below. Underline the irregular verbs. Then choose three regular verbs and three irregular verbs and write sentences in the past tense.

have	listen	take
ski	run	play
be	go	walk
throw	lose	wear
speak	carry	jump

F **BRIDGE TO WRITING**   **Personal Memories**

1. Before You Read Look at the pictures of athletes below. What
three sports are they talking about?

 2. Let's Read Read three more sports memories. Think of a **question**
you would like to ask one of the athletes.

*When I was nine years old, I played on a football team. I was an offensive guard. We
lost every game. But it was fun being on the field and wearing a football uniform.*
—**Jerry Stackhouse**, guard, Detroit Pistons
Hometown: Kinston, North Carolina

*I was a ball boy for the New York Cosmos soccer team when I was six or seven. It
was great. Soccer legend Pele was on the team. I had my picture taken with him.*
—**Tony Meola**, goalkeeper, Kansas City Wizards
Hometown: Kearney, New Jersey

*When I was ten years old, I played softball. I was the catcher, and I remember always
being afraid of getting hit by the ball.*
—**Michele Timms**, guard, Phoenix Mercury
Hometown: Melbourne, Australia

Source: *Sports Illustrated for Kids*

offensive guard—the person in a football game who
plays guard when his or her team has the ball

uniform—clothing worn by team members

softball—a game like baseball except that a larger, softer
ball is used

3. Making Content Connections Work with a partner. Choose the two sports stars from the list who you think had the *most interesting* memories. Then complete the chart below.

☐ Michele Timms   ☐ Terrell Davis   ☐ Jerry Stackhouse
☐ Jonny Moseley   ☐ Nykesha Sales   ☐ Tony Meola

Name of the sports star:	What did the person remember?	Why did the person remember this experience?
1.		
2.		

4. Expanding Your Vocabulary Learn more about sports. Work with a partner. In each row, circle the position that doesn't fit the sport.

1. Baseball

pitcher   batter   outfielder   goalkeeper

2. Football

forward   quarterback   running back   receiver

3. Basketball

guard   forward   catcher   center

G WRITING CLINIC   Personal Memories

1. Think about It A personal memory is used to describe what kind of experience?

☐ true (really happened)   ☐ imaginary (didn't really happen)

2. Focus on Organization

❶ Read three of the memories again and look at how they are organized.

> A personal memory is in the first person. It tells about the writer. It talks about just one experience.

When I was nine years old, I played on a football team. I was an offensive guard. We lost every game. But it was fun being on the field and wearing a football uniform.
—Jerry Stackhouse

> A personal memory often explains the feelings of the writer.

When I was ten years old, I played softball. I was the catcher, and I remember always being afraid of getting hit by the ball.
—Michelle Timms

> It tells us why the experience was important to the writer.

I was the first girl to play in the all-boys' summer basketball league. I ended up doing really well. Everybody was surprised, and it was a lot of fun.
—Nykesha Sales

❷ Look again at these personal memories. Talk about them with your classmates. Answer the questions that follow each personal memory.

¹*I was a ball boy for the New York Cosmos soccer team when I was six or seven.* ²*It was great.* ³*Soccer legend Pele was on the team.* ⁴*I had my picture taken with him.*
—Tony Meola

1. Which sentence describes Tony's experience?   Sentence # _____
2. Which sentence explains why Tony remembers the experience?   Sentence # _____
3. Which sentence tells us how Tony felt?   Sentence # _____

¹*When I was nine years old, I played on a football team.* ²*I was an offensive guard.* ³*We lost every game.* ⁴*But it was fun being on the field and wearing a football uniform.*
—Jerry Stackhouse

1. Which sentence describes Jerry's experience?   Sentence # _____
2. Which sentence explains why Jerry remembers the experience?   Sentence # _____
3. Which sentence tells us how Jerry felt?   Sentence # _____

3. Focus on Style Adjectives can help you describe how you felt about something. Which person below liked the game the most?

Michele

It was nice.

Tony

It was great!

Juan

It was awesome!

Think of something you liked a lot (a movie, a book, a party). Write three sentences about how you felt about it. Use different adjectives. You can use the adjectives in the box or think of some other adjectives.

fantastic	terrific	super	tremendous
wonderful	fabulous	astounding	excellent

EXAMPLE: *"The Lord of the Rings" was a fantastic movie.*

WRITER'S WORKSHOP **Personal Memories**

Help make a class book of short memories. Write your own memory for the book.

1. Getting It Out

❶ Make a chart like the one below. Fold a sheet of paper in half and then in half again to create four parts. Put a title in each part. Make a list of things you remember in each part. Circle the memory that is most important to you.

1. The first time you did something	2. A time you learned how to do something
(played baseball)	*rode a bicycle*
3. Something you did with your family or friends	4. A special event you remember
went on a camping trip	*went to my older sister's wedding*

❷ What do you remember about the experience you circled? Make a memory web of your experience. Here is Ramon's memory web. What do you think?

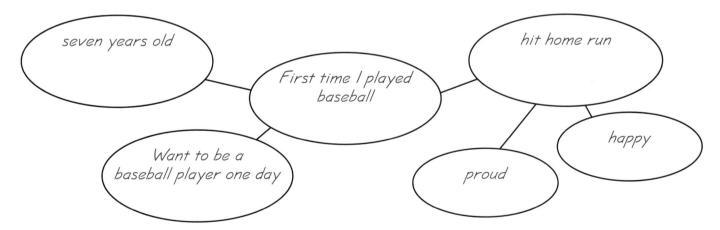

Unit 8

2. Getting It Down

❶ Turn your memory web into an outline. Use a planner like the one below.

What I did: _____

- -

How I felt: _____

- -

The reason I remember the experience: _____
_____

❷ Now turn your outline into a short memory. Here is what Ramon wrote about his memorable experience.

I remember the first time I played baseball! My first time at bat, I hit a home run! Everyone cheered. I felt happy!

Ramon describes the experience.

He explains the reason he remembers the experience so well.

He tells us how he felt.

3. Getting It Right

❶ Take a careful look at what you have written. Use this guide to revise your story.

Question to Ask	How to Check	How to Revise
1. Did I describe the experience?	<u>Underline</u> the sentence that describes the experience.	Add details so that the reader knows what you did.
2. Did I tell why I remember the experience?	Put a check mark (✓) in front of the sentence that tells why the experience was important.	Add a sentence that helps others understand why you remember the experience.
3. Did I use adjectives that tell how I felt?	Circle the adjective(s) that tell how you felt.	Add a sentence with an adjective that tells how you felt.

❷ Share your memory in a small group. Ask for feedback from your classmates.

What did you like best?

It was interesting.

How can I make it better?

Maybe tell more about how you felt.

❸ Revise your memory using the feedback from your classmates. Write a final draft of your memory.

I remember the first time I played baseball! My first time at bat, I hit a home run! Everyone cheered. I felt happy and proud!

4. Presenting It Share your memory with your classmates.

❶ Practice reading your personal memory aloud. Read it several times to a partner before you read to the class.

❷ Read your memory aloud to your classmates. Read slowly and speak clearly.

❸ Use your voice to help tell the class how you felt.

❹ Ask if anyone has any questions.

BEYOND THE UNIT

1. On Assignment Interview an adult about a memorable childhood experience. Share what you learned from the interview with your classmates.

❶ Choose someone to interview.

A family member

A teacher

Someone in your community

❷ Plan the questions you will ask. Write them on a piece of paper before the interview.

> 1. What do you remember?
> 2. Why do you still remember the event?
> 3. How did you feel at the time?

❸ Interview the person. Write down their exact words as they speak.

> What do you remember?
>
> I remember my first job. I delivered papers.

❹ Share the interview with your classmates.

SHARED READING Sometimes people write poems about memories. Read the memory poem that a student wrote.

LET'S TALK Answer the following questions.

1. What memory does the writer share with us?
2. Find the words that explain how the writer *feels*.

JUST FOR FUN Write your own memory poem.

1. Choose a memory to write about. What happened?
2. Think about how you felt when this happened.
3. Think about why you remember this event.
4. Write four or five sentences about the memory. Include information about what happened, how you felt, and why you remember the event.

Feelings Poem

Two years ago,

My grandmother died.

I was very sad.

I went to her grave.

When I think about it,

I feel very sad.

I wish my grandmother

would not die.

—Mac Babb

Source: ascd.org

grave—the place where a dead body is buried

Unit 9

Tall, Taller, Tallest

Read...

- Selections from *Hottest, Coldest, Highest, Deepest* by Steve Jenkins. Climb the tallest mountain and swim in the deepest lake in this book about the earth!

Link to Literature

- A diamante poem written by a student.

Objectives:

Reading:
- Reading information about our world
- Understanding maps and picture graphs
- Strategy: Using maps and other visuals to understand meaning
- Using information in charts
- Literature: Reading a poem

Writing:
- Writing an informational paragraph
- Writing paragraphs with a topic sentence and facts/details
- Combining sentences

Vocabulary:
- Learning geography terms: Landforms
- Learning ordinal numbers

Listening/Speaking:
- Listening to information for facts
- Comparing two places
- Giving feedback

Grammar:
- Forming comparative and superlative adjectives with –*er*, -*est*

Spelling and Phonics:
- Pronouncing words with the pattern *i* + consonant + *e*

Mount Everest

BEFORE YOU BEGIN

Talk with your classmates.

1. Look at the picture. What do you see? Help your teacher make a list.
2. Read the caption. What is the name of the mountain?
3. What do you know about Mount Everest?

A CONNECTING TO YOUR LIFE

1. Tuning In Listen to the sentences about land and water. Point your thumb up 👍 if the statement is true. Point your thumb down 👎 if it is false.

2. Talking It Over Work with a partner. Complete the captions for the pictures below with the phrases in the box.

> a. ...the hottest place in the U.S.
> b. ...the biggest lake in North America.
> c. ...the longest bridge in the world.
> d. ...the tallest volcano in the world.
> e. ...the largest island in the world.
> f. ...the coldest city in the U.S.

1. Island

Greenland is *the largest*

island in the world.

2. Lake

Lake Superior is... _____

_____

3. Desert

Death Valley is... _____

_____

4. Bridge

Akashi Kaikyo is... _____

_____

5. City

Fairbanks, Alaska, is... _____

_____

6. Volcano

Mauna Kea is... _____

_____

Read the title of this unit. What do you think the unit is probably about? Check (✓) the correct answer.

_____ 1. It's about places in the world that are fun to visit.

_____ 2. It's about places in the world that are "one of a kind."

_____ 3. It's about places in the world that are in Asia.

B GETTING READY TO READ

1. Learning New Words Read the sentences below. Try to figure out the meanings of the underlined words.

1. A foot is a measure of length or height. Mr. Valdez is six <u>feet</u> tall.
2. In many countries, people use kilometers to measure distance. In the U.S., we use <u>miles</u>, or 5,280 feet.
3. Mt. Whitney is 14,491 feet high. It takes a week to climb to the top, or the <u>summit</u>!
4. When you are standing on the beach, you are at <u>sea level</u>.
5. North America is a continent, or great area of land. The <u>continental</u> U.S. stretches from the Atlantic Ocean to the Pacific Ocean.

Match each word with the correct part of the picture below.

__d__   1. continental   _____   4. mile

_____   2. sea level   _____   5. feet

_____   3. summit

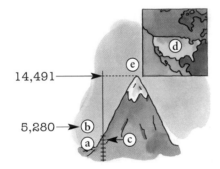

2. Talking It Over Work with a partner. How much do you know about the world? Complete the chart below. You can use an atlas.

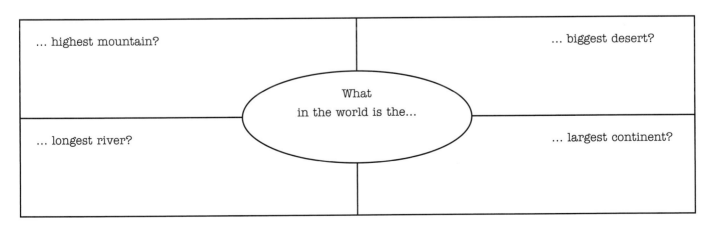

... highest mountain?

... biggest desert?

What in the world is the...

... longest river?

... largest continent?

READING STRATEGY
Using Visuals:
Use maps and other visuals to understand what you are reading.

1. Before You Read Look at the picture below. Where is this river?

☐ in the United States   ☐ in Japan   ☐ in Egypt

2. Let's Read Read the following selection. It gives important information about the longest rivers in the world. As you read, make a list of facts you didn't know.

The Nile, in Africa, is the longest river in the world. It is 4,145 (6,671 kilometers) miles long.

United States
(2,750 miles/4,426 kilometers wide)

Nile River (4,145 miles/6,671 kilometers)

Amazon River
(4,007 miles/6,448 kilometers)

Chiang Jiang River
(3,964 miles/6,379 kilometers)

Mississippi-Missouri River
(3,710 miles/5,970 kilometers)

This is a picture graph. Use it to help you understand the reading.

The Amazon River, in South America, is not as long as the Nile—it is 4,007 miles (6,448 kilometers) long—but it is considered mightier because it carries half of all the river water in the world. The Chiang Jiang (Yangtse), in Asia (3,964 miles/6,379 kilometers), and the Mississippi-Missouri, in the United States (3,710 miles/5,970 kilometers), are the world's third and fourth longest rivers.

Source: *Hottest, Coldest, Highest, Deepest* by Steve Jenkins

considered—thought to be true by most people

mightier—stronger; bigger

3. Unlocking Meaning

❶ **Finding the Main Idea** Which sentence tells the most important idea in the selection you just read. Check (✓) the correct answer.

_____ 1. The Nile is a river.

_____ 2. The Nile is the longest river on earth.

_____ 3. The Nile is 4,145 miles long.

> Here's how you say long numbers:
>
> The Nile is four thousand, one hundred forty-five miles long.

❷ **Finding Details** Work with a partner. Reread the selection on major rivers. Then complete the chart below.

Name of the River	Continent/Country	Length in Miles
Nile	Africa	4,145 miles.

❸ **Think about It** Complete the "Top Ten" list below. Put the following rivers in order from the longest to the shortest.

Mekong (2,600 miles)   Paraná (2,796 miles)   Congo (2,900 miles)

~~Ob-Irtysh (3,362 miles)~~   Lena (2,734 miles)   Huang (3,395 miles)

The Ten Longest Rivers

1. Nile (4,145 miles)
2. Amazon (4,007 miles)
3. Chiang Jiang (3,964 miles)
4. Mississippi-Missouri (3,710 miles)
5. _Ob-Irtysh (3,362 miles)_

6. _____
7. _____
8. _____
9. _____
10. _____

❹ **Before You Move On** Think about your own community. Write answers to the following questions.

1. What is the tallest building in your community?

   _____

2. What is the longest street or road?

   _____

3. What is the largest park?

   _____

D WORD WORK

1. Word Detective Look at these people in line. Match the descriptions on the left with the positions on the right.

1. man in the orange cap
2. girl in the blue cap
3. boy in the purple cap
4. boy in the green cap
5. girl in the pink cap
6. girl in the brown cap
7. woman in the black cap
8. boy in the red cap

a. first
b. second
c. third
d. fourth
e. fifth
f. seventh
g. eighth
h. tenth

2. Word Study Each number that you use to count (cardinal numbers, like *one*) also has a number that you use to show the order of things (ordinal numbers, like *first*). Most ordinal numbers end in *–th* or *–eth*.

SPECIAL WORDS FOR ORDER	MOST ORDINAL NUMBERS END IN *–TH*	SOMETIMES THE ORIGINAL SPELLING CHANGES
one → first	four → fourth	nine → ninth
two → second	six → sixth	five → fifth
three → third	thirteen → thirteenth	twenty → twentieth

Beginning with twenty-one/ twenty-first, put a hyphen between the words.

Write the cardinal number for each ordinal number below.

fortieth	seventeenth	ninth	sixty-fifth
forty			
fifty-first	eightieth	eleventh	sixth
_____	_____	_____	_____

SPELLING AND PHONICS:
To do this activity, go to page 186.

3. Word Play Work with a partner. Write the ordinal number for each cardinal number below.

seven	fifty	one
seventh		
three	five	ten
_____	_____	_____

E **GRAMMAR**   Comparatives and Superlatives: *-er, -est*

🎧 **1. Listen Up** Listen to each sentence. Point your thumb up 👍 if it sounds correct. Point your thumb down 👎 if it sounds wrong.

👍👎 1. Mt. Everest is more tall than Mt. Whitney.

👍👎 2. The Nile is longer than the Amazon.

👍👎 3. The Amazon is more shorter than the Nile.

👍👎 4. Fairbanks is more cold than Los Angeles.

👍👎 5. Rome is warmer than London.

👍👎 6. Lake Superior is more bigger than Lake Michigan.

2. Learn the Rule To compare things, you need to use comparative and superlative adjectives. Read and learn the following rules. Then do Activity 1 again.

COMPARATIVE AND SUPERLATIVE ADJECTIVES

a. When you want to compare two people or things, you often add *–er* + *than* to the adjective.	b. When you describe how someone or something is one of a kind, you add *–est*. *The* must come before the adjective.

The Sears Tower is tall.
The Sears Tower is tall**er than** the Empire State Building.

Maria is fast.
Maria is fast**er than** Rumiko.

The Sears Tower is taller than all other buildings in the U.S.
The Sears Tower is **the** tall**est** building in the U.S.

Maria is faster than everybody on the team.
Maria is **the** fast**est** person on the team.

3. Practice the Rule Work with a partner. Look around for items or people you can compare. Then write five sentences using comparative and superlative adjectives.

EXAMPLE: *Marco is the tallest person in class.*

1. _____
2. _____
3. _____
4. _____
5. _____

F BRIDGE TO WRITING

READING STRATEGY
Using Visuals:
Use maps and other visuals to understand what you are reading.

1. Before You Read Write the name of the highest mountain you can think of. Compare your idea with a partner's.

Highest mountain: _____

2. Let's Read Read about Mount Everest. Be ready to identify and share with the class one fact you didn't know before the reading.

Mount Everest is the highest mountain in the world. Its peak is 29,028 feet (8,848 meters) above sea level.

Compare the information in the picture graph with the information in the reading.

Mt. Everest
29,028 ft.

Denali
20,320 ft.

Mt. Whitney
14,491 ft.

The highest mountain in North America is Mount McKinley (also called Denali), in Alaska, at 20,320 feet (6,194 meters). Mount Whitney, in California, is the highest peak in the continental United States. Its summit is 14,491 feet (4,417 meters) above sea level.

Source: *Hottest, Coldest, Highest, Deepest* by Steve Jenkins

peak—the top of a very tall mountain

3. Making Content Connections You have read about two places in the world that are *unique* (one of a kind). Work with a partner. Complete the chart below. Use complete sentences.

	The Nile	Mt. Everest
Why is it unique?	It is the longest river in the world.	
Where is it located?		
What is one important fact about it?		

4. Expanding Your Vocabulary Learn the names of more landforms. Work with a partner. Match each word with a picture.

a.    b.    c.

d.    e. 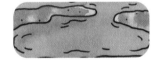   f.

___c___   1. bay: an area of water with land around most of it (smaller than a gulf)

_____   2. continent: one of the seven great areas of land: Africa, Antarctica, Asia, Australia, Europe, North America, and South America

_____   3. gulf: an area of ocean with land around most of it (larger than a bay)

_____   4. peninsula: land with water on three sides

_____   5. prairie: a large area of flat land with tall grasses and few trees

_____   6. valley: a low place between two mountains

G | WRITING CLINIC

1. Think about It Read the information about the Nile again.

> **The Nile, in Africa, is the longest river in the world. It is 4,145 miles (6,671 kilometers) long.**

Where would you find information like this? Check (✓) all of the correct answers.

_____ 1. in a magazine   _____ 4. in an encyclopedia

_____ 2. in a textbook   _____ 5. in a book of poetry

_____ 3. in a story   _____ 6. in your student handbook

2. Focus on Organization

The sentence in green is the topic sentence. The sentence in yellow is a fact. It supports the topic sentence.

❶ Read the short paragraph about Mt. Everest again. What is the main idea? Tell a partner what you think.

> **Mount Everest is the highest mountain in the world. Its peak is 29,028 feet (8,848 meters) above sea level.**

❷ Match each topic sentence on the left with the correct fact on the right.

1. Denali is the highest mountain in North America.
2. Tutunendo, Colombia, is the wettest place on earth.
3. The deepest place in the ocean is the Mariana Trench.
4. The snowiest place on earth is Mount Rainier, in Washington State.
5. The Amazon is the second longest river in the world.
6. The Atacama Desert, in Chile, is the driest spot on earth.

a. Over 400 inches of rain fall every year.
b. One year, more than 1,200 feet of snow fell there.
c. It is 20,320 feet high.
d. It is over 4,000 miles in length.
e. It hasn't rained there in 400 years.
f. It is 36,202 feet deep.

❸ Pretend you wanted to write a paragraph with these three sentences in it.

Mount Washington is in New Hampshire.

Mount Washington is the windiest place in North America.

Winds sometimes blow over 200 miles per hour there.

Complete the outline with the sentences from above. Write the sentence that would be a good topic sentence on the top line. Write sentences that give facts about the topic on the remaining two lines.

Topic sentence: _____

Fact: _____

Fact: _____

2. Focus on Style

❶ Two sentences can often be combined (put together) to make an expanded sentence. Sometimes an expanded sentence is easier to read than two shorter sentences that repeat information.

The Nile is the longest river in the world.
The Nile is in Africa.
The Nile, *in Africa*, is the longest river in the world.

❷ Combine each of the following pairs of sentences. Write each of the new combined sentences on a separate sheet of paper.

1. Mount Everest is the tallest mountain in the world.
   Mount Everest is in Nepal.

2. Tokyo is the largest city in the world.
   Tokyo is in Japan.

3. Greenland is the largest island in the world.
   Greenland is in the Atlantic Ocean.

4. Mauna Loa is the largest volcano in the world.
   Mauna Loa is in Hawaii.

5. The Sears Tower is the tallest building in the U.S.
   The Sears Tower is in Chicago.

6. The Amazon is the widest river in the world.
   The Amazon is in South America.

H WRITER'S WORKSHOP — Short Reports: Our World

Help your class write an atlas, called "Wonders of the World." Make a page for the atlas. Your page should include each of the following items:

☐ a drawing of the place you choose

☐ a short paragraph (two or three sentences) that tells why the place is one of a kind

☐ a map or a picture graph that helps your reader understand the information even better

1. Getting It Out

❶ Choose a place to write about. Look at the pictures below for ideas or choose another place you know about.

The hottest place on earth

Al Aziziyah

The coldest place on earth

Vostok

The world's highest waterfall

Angel Falls

The world's deepest lake

Lake Baikal

❷ Learn more about the place you have chosen. Use this chart or do your own research on a different place.

Place	Country/Continent	Important Facts
Al Aziziyah	Libya (Africa)	Town in the Sahara Desert Hottest place on earth Shade temperature of 141° F (61°C) once recorded there Even hotter than the Mojave Desert in California
Vostok	Antarctica	Near the South Pole Coldest place on earth Temperature of 129° below zero (−129° F/−89° C) once recorded there Average temperature at the South Pole is −58° F (−50° C)
Angel Falls	Venezuela (South America)	World's highest waterfall 3,212 feet (979 meters) high Higher than Niagara Falls in the U.S. (180 feet/55 meters high) Discovered in 1935 by explorer James C. Angel
Lake Baikal	Russia (Asia)	World's deepest lake Deepest spot: 5,134 feet (1,565 meters) Over 25 million years old (the world's oldest lake) Contains 20% of the earth's fresh water

CONNECT TO THE WEB. CHECK IT OUT:

For links to Web sites in different subject areas, go to the American Library Association's "Great Web Sites for Kids:"
www.ala.org/parentspage/greatsites

── MINI-LESSON ──
Using Exclamation Points:
When a sentence is especially interesting or really amazing, use an exclamation point.

It's even hotter than the Mojave Desert!

■ ■ ■

2. Getting It Down

❶ Draw a picture of the place you have chosen.

❷ Add words to explain and describe the picture. Complete the outline below.

Topic sentence: _____

Fact: _____

Fact: _____

❸ Turn your outline into a paragraph. Here is what Rosita wrote. What do you think?

*The paragraph has a **topic sentence**.*

*Each **fact** relates to the topic sentence.*

Al Aziziyah, in Libya, is the hottest place on earth.

The temperature in the shade can get over 140°F (60°C).

It's even **more hot** than the Mojave Desert!

Oops! This should be "hotter."

❹ Add a map or a picture graph to help your reader understand what you have written.

3. Getting It Right Look carefully at what you have written. Use this guide to revise your paragraph.

Question to Ask	How to Check	How to Revise
1. Does my paragraph have a topic sentence?	<u>Underline</u> your topic sentence.	Add a sentence that tells the main idea.
2. Do the facts relate to the topic sentence?	Put a check mark (✔) in front of each sentence that gives a fact.	Add sentences that give facts. Take out sentences that do not.
3. Do I use expanded sentences to avoid repeating information?	Look at the examples on page 157. Are there any sentences I can combine?	Try putting two sentences together to make one.

4. Presenting It Share the page you have written with your classmates.

❶ Begin by showing the picture of the place you chose and naming it.

❷ Read your paragraph aloud. Read slowly and speak clearly.

❸ Ask for feedback from your classmates.

 I learned a lot about the hottest place on earth.

 The map is easy to read!

You spoke slowly and clearly. Your presentation was easy to listen to.

1. On Assignment A picture graph uses pictures and numbers to compare two or more similar things. The picture graph below compares three of the world's tallest buildings.

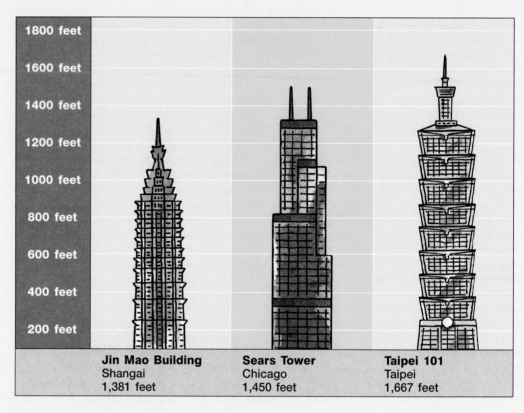

| | Jin Mao Building Shangai 1,381 feet | Sears Tower Chicago 1,450 feet | Taipei 101 Taipei 1,667 feet |

Make a picture graph that compares two or more things at your school or home.

❶ Decide what you will compare.

How high?

How long?

How wide?

How deep?

❷ Measure each object.

❸ Make a graph with inches or feet along one axis.

❹ Draw each object in your graph.

❺ Add a caption under each object explaining what it is.

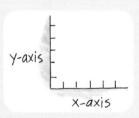

SHARED READING Read the diamante poem written by an ESL student. A diamante poem is shaped like a diamond and has seven lines.

LET'S TALK Answer the following questions and do the activity.

1. How many lines does the poem have? How many words are in each line?

2. For each line, write the letter of the type of word that is used in that line.

   ___*a*___ Line 1
   _____ Line 2
   _____ Line 3
   _____ Line 4
   _____ Line 5
   _____ Line 6
   _____ Line 7

   a. Noun
   b. Adjective
   c. Verb + –*ing*

3. How are line 1 and line 7 connected to each other?

4. Why is the title of the poem, "The Earth"?

The Earth
By Ivan

[1]Mountain
[2]High, rocky
[3]Flying, looking, killing
[4]Eagle, power, fear, rabbit
[5]Living, moving, making noise
[6]Deep, beautiful
[7]Valley

Source: darkwing.uoregon.edu

What Do You Think?

Read...

- Selections from opinion columns published by *Sports Illustrated for Kids*. Read students' opinions on interesting issues!

Link to Literature

- "Point of View," a poem by Shel Silverstein.

Objectives:

Reading:

- Evaluating students' opinions on various issues
- Strategy: Evaluating ideas as you read
- Literature: Responding to a poem

Writing:

- Writing an opinion column based on interviews
- Using complete sentences
- Using quoted words

Vocabulary:

- Recognizing word families: Related nouns and adjectives
- Learning language that expresses opinion

Listening/Speaking:

- Listening and responding to two sides of an issue
- Interviewing: Asking others about their opinions
- Sharing opinions and giving reasons to support an opinion

Grammar:

- Making comparisons: *as...as, more...than*

Spelling and Phonics:

- Spelling the /ī/ sound as in *my* and *high*

Yes or no?

BEFORE YOU BEGIN

Talk with your classmates.

1. Look at the two pictures. What do you think is happening?
2. If you are a **boy**: Should a girl play on a boys' sports team? Circle *Yes* or *No*.
   If you are a **girl**: Should a boy play on a girls' team? Circle *Yes* or *No*.
3. Help your teacher tally, or count, the boys' answers and the girls' answers.

A CONNECTING TO YOUR LIFE

1. Tuning In Listen to Juan and Lori talk about TV. Who do you agree with, Juan or Lori?

2. Talking It Over Read the questions below. Check (✓) *Yes* or *No* for each question.

	Yes	No
1. Is watching a lot of TV bad for you?		
2. Are girls smarter than boys?		
3. Does school get out too early?		
4. Do kids have too much homework?		
5. Should kids have to take PE?		

Choose one of the questions above. Write the reason you answered *Yes* or *No*. Share your reason with your classmates.

Question: _____

Answer: _____

Reason: _____

_____

_____

_____

Read the title. What do you think the unit is probably about? Check (✓) the correct answer.

_____ 1. It's about interesting facts about the world.

_____ 2. It's about issues, or questions, students have ideas about.

_____ 3. It's about learning how to think better.

B GETTING READY TO READ

1. Learning New Words Read the vocabulary words and their definitions.

action—exciting things that happen

different—not like something or someone else

allowed—having permission to do something

skill—the ability to do something very well

challenge—something new or difficult that requires skill

out of style—not in fashion or popular anymore

Complete the sentences with the vocabulary words above.

1. Susanna came to the U.S. from Germany two weeks ago. It is a _____ for her to speak English.
2. Maria is the best player on the soccer team. She has a lot of _____.
3. When students are taking a test, they are not _____ to talk.
4. Sonia has bright blue hair. She looks _____ from most other kids.
5. Mr. Johnson wears old-fashioned clothes. His clothing is _____.
6. Tran likes movies with car chases and fighting. He likes movies with a lot of _____.

2. Talking It Over Work in a small group. Talk about reasons for answering "yes" and reasons for answering "no" for each question in the chart below. Then complete the chart.

Question	Reasons for answering "yes"	Reasons for answering "no"
1. Is watching a lot of TV bad for you?	You don't have time to do your homework.	You can learn a lot from TV.
2. Are girls smarter than boys?		
3. Does school get out too early?		
4. Do kids have too much homework?		
5. Should kids have to take PE?		

READING STRATEGY

Evaluating Ideas:
When you evaluate ideas, you decide whether you agree with them or not.

The Cincinnati Red Stockings were the first professional baseball team. The team began playing in 1869.

'n' is short for "and."

C READING TO LEARN   Opinion Columns

1. Before You Read What do you think is most Americans' favorite sport? Tell a partner.

2. Let's Read Read this opinion column. Kids shared their opinions, or ideas, on baseball. As you read, decide what *your own* opinion is. Be ready to share your ideas.

Is Baseball Still America's Favorite Sport?

YES!	NO!
"Baseball is so good, you can't even begin to describe it. There's nothing like the crack of the bat or the smell of hot dogs." **—Nick,** *sent by e-mail*	"Americans are more interested in seeing someone dunk than hit a home run. This is especially true for kids." **—Kelsey J.,** *Sioux City, Iowa*
"In every city, kids are playing baseball. It's all over the newspapers, TV, magazines, and books." **—Brett R.,** *Bakersfield, California*	"People want to watch fast-paced sports, like football and basketball. Baseball is out of style." **—Jeff V.,** *Bartlesville, Oklahoma*
"Baseball is like rock 'n' roll: It will never die." **—Chance C.,** *Grapevine, Texas*	"In baseball, 95 percent of the time there is no action. Only a few people want to watch that." **—Talia S.,** *Merion, Pennsylvania*
"It doesn't matter how old the game is, people still like baseball a lot." **—Yegor D.,** *Cleveland, Ohio*	

Source: Sports Illustrated for Kids

---

crack—a loud noise that sounds like something breaking

bat—a long wooden stick used for hitting a baseball

all over—everywhere you look

still—continuing until now or until a particular time

dunk—to push a basketball through the hoop at close range

home run—a long hit in baseball in which the hitter is able to run around all the bases and score a point

fast-paced—having lots of action

3. Unlocking Meaning

❶ **Finding the Main Idea** In this selection, what is each writer talking about? Check (✓) the correct answer.

_____ 1. reasons that baseball is so popular

_____ 2. his or her own opinion about baseball

_____ 3. reasons that most people like fast-paced sports like football

❷ **Finding Details** Listen as your teacher reads each statement below. Point your thumb up if it supports the "YES!" opinion in the reading on the previous page. Point your thumb down if it supports the "NO!" opinion.

👍👎 1. Read the sports page, and all you will find are stories about baseball.

👍👎 2. Baseball will always be Number 1 for most people.

👍👎 3. Most Americans, especially kids, like basketball more than baseball.

👍👎 4. Baseball is a boring game because it is so slow.

👍👎 5. Even though it is an old game, baseball is still popular.

👍👎 6. Baseball is a game that mostly old people like to watch.

❸ **Think about It** Talk with a partner. In the reading, which kid gives the best reason for his or her opinion? Why?

❹ **Before You Move On** Think of one more reason for answering *Yes* or *No* to the question about baseball.

D WORD WORK

1. Word Detective Words that look alike, or almost alike, often belong to the same word family. Match the noun on the left with its correct adjective form on the right.

1. difference   a. skillful
2. interest   b. long
3. skill   c. different
4. length   d. beautiful
5. beauty   e. friendly
6. friend   f. high
7. height   g. interesting

2. Word Study Words in the same word family look alike, but they have different meanings and different jobs in a sentence. Work with a partner. Choose one noun/adjective pair from above and write a sentence for each word in the pair.

EXAMPLE: *interest/interesting*
               Juan has many <u>interests</u>.
               Juan is an <u>interesting</u> person.

3. Word Play Work with a partner. Write the missing nouns and adjectives. You can use your dictionary.

┌─ **SPELLING AND PHONICS:** ─┐
To do this activity, go to
page 186.
      ■ ■ ■

Noun	Adjective
1. _____	loveable
2. music	_____
3. salt	_____
4. _____	colorful
5. width	_____
6. _____	dangerous
7. _____	legendary

Now choose three noun/adjective pairs and write a sentence for each word.

1. noun: _____
    adjective: _____
2. noun: _____
    adjective: _____
3. noun: _____
    adjective: _____

E GRAMMAR   Comparisons: *As...As, More...Than*

1. Listen Up Listen to each sentence. Point your thumb up 👍 if it sounds correct. Point your thumb down 👎 if it sounds wrong.

👍👎 1. Juan is as intelligent as Carlos.

👍👎 3. The Nile is longer than the Amazon.

👍👎 2. Carlos is more better at sports than Juan.

👍👎 4. A lion is ferociouser than a tiger.

2. Learn the Rule Certain words in a sentence show that two things are being compared. Read the following rules. Then do Activity 1 again.

COMPARISONS: *AS...AS, MORE...THAN*	
a. When you compare two things that are equal, or the same, use *as...as*.	
Girls' sports are important. Boys' sports are important.	*Girls' sports are **as** important **as** boys' sports.*
b. When you compare two things that are different, use *than*. Add *–er* to most adjectives to make them comparative. Irregular comparative adjectives have their own special form.	
*Mt. Whitney is tall. Mr. Everest is tall**er**.* *Sausage pizza is good. Pepperoni pizza is **better**.*	*Mt. Everest is tall**er than** Mt. Whitney.* *Pepperoni pizza is **better than** sausage pizza.*
c. For adjectives that have three or more syllables, use *more...than* to compare two things that are different.	
Senator Smith is important. President Chan is more important.	*President Chan is **more** important **than** Senator Smith.*

3. Practice the Rule Complete the sentences below using the adjectives in parentheses.

1. Juan and Carlos are both 6 feet tall. Juan is (tall) ___as tall as___ Carlos.

2. I like chocolate ice cream and vanilla ice cream. Chocolate ice cream is (good) _____ vanilla.

3. Lori is 13. Maria is 15. Lori is (young) _____ Maria.

4. English is easy for me, but math is difficult. Math is (difficult) _____ English.

5. My mother and father are 37 years old. My mother is (old) _____ my father.

F BRIDGE TO WRITING   Opinion Columns

1. Before You Read Are there things that boys should do only with boys and girls should do only with girls? Talk with a partner.

2. Let's Read As you read, write each person's name on a piece of paper. Then draw a face next to the name showing how you feel about their opinion.

☺ = Good point!   ☺ = Not sure   ☹ = Silly idea

> *Avery uses "would" instead of "will" because boys don't really play on girls' teams. Use "would" for imaginary situations.*

Should boys be allowed to play on girls' sports teams?

YES!	NO!
"Girls' sports take as much skill as boys' sports. So what difference does it make if a boy plays on a girls' team?" —**Annie B.,** *Cleveland Heights, Ohio*	"The girls would not feel comfortable playing with one boy, and the one boy would not feel comfortable playing with the girls." —**Thomas P.,** *Eugene, Oregon*
"If boys played with girls' teams, it would make the games more interesting." —**Avery M.,** *Iowa City, Iowa*	"Boys play too hard and rough. Also, they wouldn't be allowed in the girls' locker room." —**Karissa E.,** *Billings, Montana*
"Boys and girls can help each other learn different sports." —**Ryan G.,** *Reno, Nevada*	"A boy would feel embarrassed in front of his friends if he was on a team with girls." —**Vince M.,** *Kenosha, Wisconsin*
"A boy can be on a girls' sports team—if he can handle the challenge." —**Annie S.,** *Oakton, Virginia*	"Girls don't need boys' help. Anything boys can do, girls can do better." —**Whitney-Ann S.,** *New Bedford, Massachusetts*

Source: *Sports Illustrated for Kids*

comfortable—at ease and relaxed

embarrassed—feeling shy or ashamed in front of other people

3. Making Content Connections You have read kids' opinions about two questions. Work with a partner. Think about the opinions you have read and complete the chart below.

	Baseball still Number 1?	Boys on girls' teams?
What is the best "Yes" reason?		
What is the best "No" reason?		

4. Expanding Your Vocabulary Give your opinion on one of the issues you have read about. Role play with a partner. You can start with one of the phrases below.

In my opinion, . . .

I believe that . . .

I feel that . . .

I think that . . .

It's my opinion that . . .

G WRITING CLINIC

1. Think about It In which part of a newspaper or magazine would you usually find an opinion column?

☐ sports section   ☐ editorial page/letters from readers

☐ world and national news   ☐ want ads

2. Focus on Organization

❶ Read again what kids said about boys playing on girls' teams.

The column begins with a question.

Yes opinions come first.

The person often gives a reason for his or her opinion.

Quotation marks go around a person's actual words.

Sometimes the person's opinion makes you laugh.

Should boys be allowed to play on girls' sports teams?

YES!

"Girls' sports take as much skill as boys' sports. So what difference does it make if a boy plays on a girls' team?"

—**Annie B.,** *Cleveland Heights, Ohio*

"If boys played with girls' teams, it would make the games more interesting."

—**Avery M.,** *Iowa City, Iowa*

"Boys and girls can help each other learn different sports."

—**Ryan G.,** *Reno, Nevada*

"A boy can be on a girls' sports team—if he can handle the challenge."

—**Annie S.,** *Oakton, Virginia*

❷ Reread the *No* opinions. List three reasons kids give for their opinions. Use your own words.

> ### NO!
>
> "The girls would not feel comfortable playing with one boy, and the one boy would not feel comfortable playing with the girls."
>
> **—Thomas P.,** *Eugene, Oregon*
>
> "Boys play too hard and rough. Also, they wouldn't be allowed in the girls' locker room."
>
> **—Karissa E.,** *Billings, Montana*
>
> "A boy would feel embarrassed in front of his friends if he was on a team with girls."
>
> **—Vince M.,** *Kenosha, Wisconsin*
>
> "Girls don't need boys' help. Anything boys can do, girls can do better."
>
> **—Whitney-Ann S.,** *New Bedford, Massachusetts*

3. Focus on Style

❶ People's actual words are interesting to read. Quotation marks tell you that you are reading exactly what a person said.

> *"If a boy plays on a girls' team, it's like cheating on a test. Boys are stronger and faster. Only girls' scores should count."*
> *–Steven H., Florida*

❷ Practice using quotation marks. Rewrite each person's actual words.

1.

Girls are smarter than boys.

Sara Dubois

2.

Kids don't have enough homework.

Mr. Torres, parent

3.

Watching a lot of TV is bad for you!

Ms. Fields, teacher

4.

Kids have too much homework.

Lori Chang

5.

Kids shouldn't have to take PE.

Stefan Kopec

6.

The school day is too short.

Ms. Chan, school principal

H WRITER'S WORKSHOP   Opinion Columns

Imagine that you are a reporter for your school newspaper. Your job is to interview other students for "The Question Kid," a weekly opinion column.

1. Getting It Out

❶ Choose an interesting question to ask students. Use one of the following questions, or think of your own. Your question should:

- be interesting.
- have a "yes" or "no" answer.

1.

Does school get out too early?

2.

Do students have too much homework?

3.

Is watching a lot of TV bad for you?

4.

Are girls smarter than boys?

5.

Should students have to take PE?

6.

Make your own question!

❷ Make a note-taking sheet like the one below.

Question: Should students have to take PE?

YES:

NO:

❸ Interview six to eight classmates or other friends and family members. Write down each person's *exact words*!

Question: Should students have to take PE?

YES:
Yes. Students should exercise every day.

NO:

❹ Put the person's name and grade, or position if it is a teacher or the principal, in parentheses next to his or her words.

Question: Should students have to take PE?

YES:
Yes. Students should exercise every day. (Juan Ortiz, grade 9)

NO:

These marks are called parentheses.

❺ Listen to the tape or CD. Write down each person's answers. Write their *exact* words.

2. Getting It Down

❶ Make an outline like the one below.

Question: *Should students have to take PE?*	

YES:	NO:
Name: *Juan Ortiz, grade 9* Opinion: *Students should exercise every day.*	Name: _____ Opinion: _____
Name: _____ Opinion: _____	Name: _____ Opinion: _____
Name: _____ Opinion: _____	Name: _____ Opinion: _____

MINI-LESSON

Using Periods with Quotation Marks:

Put periods inside quotation marks:

"PE teaches you to play by the rules."

❷ Draft your opinion column. Put quotation marks around each person's words. Here is part of what Lori wrote. What do you think?

Lori repeats the question.

The Question Kid: Should kids have to take PE?

YES!	NO!
"Students should exercise every day" —*Juan Ortiz*, Grade 9 "PE teaches you to play by the rules." —*Lourdes Aguiao*, Grade 9 "PE helps build strong muscles" —*Arnulf Schwarz*, Grade 8	"Taking showers with others is embarrassing" —*Paris Valdez*, Grade 7

She puts quotation marks around each student's words. She names each student and tells the grade.

3. Getting It Right Look carefully at your opinion column. Use this guide to revise your work.

Question to Ask	How to Check	How to Revise
1. Do I restate the question at the top of the column?	Put a star (★) next to the question.	Make sure that the word order is right and that you use a question mark.
2. Did I report at least three "yes" opinions and three "no" opinions?	Put a number next to each opinion.	Interview more people.
3. Did I report each person's exact words?	Show each person the words you wrote down.	Change the words to get them right.
4. Did I put quotation marks around each person's words?	Check to see that quotation marks begin and end each quotation and that the period is inside.	Add quotation marks. Change the location of the period.

4. Presenting It Share your opinion column with your classmates.

❶ Form a group with other students who asked the same question. Decide who will read first, then second, then third, and so forth.

❷ Read all of the *Yes* opinions to the class. Be sure that everybody has a chance to give a report.

❸ Then read the *No* opinions.

❹ Ask if anyone wants to add another idea or opinion.

1. On Assignment Read the following letters that students wrote to *Junior Scholastic Magazine*.

❶ *Junior Scholastic* asked its readers for their opinions about year-round school. Read letters from two students:

Dear Editor:
    I think the new school year would be a good change. We would still get our vacations, but we would get it at different times of the year. It would also keep us fresh and on the ball because during summer vacation we just stop thinking of school.

Kasey Jasper

Dear Editor:
    Summer is a time for us kids to relax and clear our minds of the stress and pressure of the school world. It also gives us time to maybe take a vacation and have more outdoor experiences. We can also spend more time with our families.

Michelle Walter

Source: Letters written by students at Broad Meadows Middle School in Quincy, Massachusetts

year-round school—schools that are open all year. Students have more short vacations rather than a long summer vacation.

on the ball—able to think quickly

stress—worries that keep you from relaxing

pressure—a feeling that you have too much work and other things to do

outdoor experiences—activities like camping and fishing

❷ Work with a partner. Make a list of the reasons kids give for their opinions about year-round schools. Use your own words.

❸ Now think of an issue you have an opinion about. Write a short letter to the editor of your school newspaper. Use the form below to help with your letter.

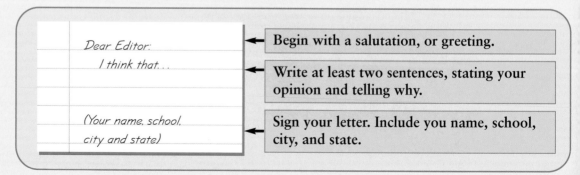

Dear Editor:
    I think that...

(Your name, school, city and state)

→ Begin with a salutation, or greeting.

→ Write at least two sentences, stating your opinion and telling why.

→ Sign your letter. Include you name, school, city, and state.

 **SHARED READING** Read this poem about point of view. It's by Shel Silverstein.

LET'S TALK

1. What is the turkey's "point of view" about Thanksgiving dinner?
2. Why is it a good idea to look at things from another point of view?
3. Why is the poem clever and funny?

JUST FOR FUN Think of a situation from your daily life. Imagine it from the point of view of an object or a thing. Write a poem about it.

ABOUT THE AUTHOR

Shel Silverstein was born in Chicago and died in 1999. He wrote nearly twenty-five books, published in 30 different languages. *Where the Sidewalk Ends*, *A Light in the Attic*, and *Falling Up* are three of his most famous collections of poetry and drawings.

POINT OF VIEW

Thanksgiving dinner's sad and thankless
Christmas dinner's dark and blue
When you stop and try to see it
From the turkey's point of view.

Sunday dinner isn't sunny
Easter feasts are just bad luck
When you see it from the viewpoint
Of a chicken or a duck.

Oh how I once loved tuna salad
Pork and lobsters, lamb chops too
Till I stopped and looked at dinner
From the dinner's point of view.

Source: *Where the Sidewalk Ends*, by Shel Silverstein

thankless—unpleasant and without thankful feelings

blue—sad

sunny—happy

feast—a large meal, often for many people

viewpoint—what someone believes or thinks

lobster—an ocean shellfish with large claws

chop—a piece of meat

till—until

Spelling and Phonics Activities

UNIT 1

Spelling and Phonics The letter *i* can sound different, depending on the word it is in. Listen to these words.

pride   winner

Complete the chart below. Put each word from the box in the correct column.

like	wild	picture	nice
stupid	in	I'm	live

/ī/ as in *pride*	/i/ as in *winner*
like	

UNIT 2

Spelling and Phonics The letter *a* can sound different depending on the word it is in. Listen to these words.

walk   candy   man   lawn

Complete the chart below. Put each word from the box in the correct column.

draw	paw	eyeball
glass	swan	hat
wall	avalanche	talk

/a/ as in *candy*	/ô/ as in *walk*
	draw

Spelling and Phonics The letter *o* can be pronounced in different ways when a consonant + *e* follows it. Listen to the following words.

role   come

Complete the chart below. Put each word from the box in the correct column.

home	love	some	stove
shove	Coke	go	rope
done	close	none	one

/ō/ as in *role*	/ŭ/ as in *come*
home	

UNIT 4

 Spelling and Phonics The consonant sound /s/ can be spelled in many ways. Listen to the following words.

house   city   kiss   listen

Supply the missing letters for each of the following incomplete words. Use your dictionary to check your work.

a. Eeek! I see a mou_s_e!

b. Do you mi__ me?

c. I live in San Fran__isco.

d. I am taking five cla__es.

e. Juan blew the whi__le.

f. Do you celebrate Chri__mas?

g. Five __ents equals a nickel.

h. What's your addre__?

i. I see my fa__e in the mirror.

🎧 **Spelling and Phonics** The letter *a* can sound different depending on the word it is in. Listen to these words.

cat   snake   yawn

Complete the chart below. Put each word from the box in the correct column.

have	mantis	male	Africa
swallow	alligator	talk	small
praying	Asia	gigantic	anaconda

/a/ as in *cat*	/ā/ as in *snake*	/ô/ as in *yawn*
have		

UNIT 6

🎧 **Spelling and Phonics** The consonant sound /k/ can be spelled in many ways. Listen to these words.

cool   school   kid   kick   quick

Supply the missing letters for each of the following incomplete words. Use your dictionary to check your work.

a. Juan loves to _c_ook.

b. My stoma__ hurts.

c. The paper costs a __uarter.

d. Can you __eep a secret?

e. I feel si__!

f. Do you have a __uestion?

g. I feel lu__y.

h. __ould you help me?

i. What's the s__edule?

UNIT 7

🎧 **Spelling and Phonics** *Digraphs* are two consonants that we put together to make just one sound. Listen to the following sentence. Look at the circled digraph in the underlined word.

My favorite ice cream is (ch)ocolate.

Each of the following words has a digraph. Say each word, and then circle the digraph.

di(sh)	what	weather	with
pharmacy	cheese	shoe	when
think	either	sing	chicken
chorus	who	thank	photo

UNIT 8

🎧 **Spelling and Phonics** Sometimes a consonant (or consonant cluster) is silent. Listen to the sentence. Which consonant is silent in the underlined word?

Johnny tore ligaments in his <u>knee</u>.

Each of the following words has a silent consonant or consonants. Say each word, and then circle the silent consonant or consonants.

(k)now	ghost	listen	sign
eight	wrap	right	knock
write	comb	often	wreck
island	spaghetti	dumb	rhyme

🎧 **Spelling and Phonics** The letter *i* can be pronounced in different ways when a consonant + *e* follows it. Listen to the following words.

Nile   river   magazine

Copy the chart below on a separate piece of paper. Put all the words in the following table with the same *i* sound together in the chart.

gasoline	line	time	prize
smile	five	like	tangerine
give	fifth	shiver	bike

/ī/ as in *Nile*	/i/ as in *river*	/ē/ as in *magazine*
smile		

🎧 **Spelling and Phonics** The sound /ī/ can be spelled many ways. Listen to the following words.

line   die   my   high

Supply the missing letters for each of the following incomplete words. Use your dictionary to check your work.

a. Baseball is out of st_y_le.

b. Tim has n__ne brothers!

c. I have to t__ my shoe.

d. Do you like apple p__?

e. Juan was born in Jul__.

f. Maria m__t go with us.

g. Snow is usually wh__te.

h. Tran is a n__ce guy.

i. I go to bed at n__t.

ChecBrics*

ChecBric for "Me" Collage

Focus	Overall rating
Organization _____ I used both words and pictures. _____ I placed my pictures in an interesting way.	_____ 4 = Wow! _____ 3 = Strong _____ 2 = Some strengths _____ 1 = Needs work
Content My collage tells about... _____ me. _____ my family and friends. _____ what I like. _____ what I like to do.	_____ 4 = Wow! _____ 3 = Strong _____ 2 = Some strengths _____ 1 = Needs work
Style _____ I used pictures and photos. _____ I used words to tell about me. _____ I used different sizes of letters and words. _____ My collage is nice to look at.	_____ 4 = Wow! _____ 3 = Strong _____ 2 = Some strengths _____ 1 = Needs work
Grammar and mechanics _____ I spelled the words correctly. _____ I capitalized people's names.	_____ 4 = Wow! _____ 3 = Strong _____ 2 = Some strengths _____ 1 = Needs work

*ChecBric name and concept created by Larry Lewin.

ChecBric for Signs

Focus	Overall rating
Organization ____ The signs on each page have the same job. ____ I used pictures with my signs. ____ Each page has a caption.	____ 4 = Wow! ____ 3 = Strong ____ 2 = Some strengths ____ 1 = Needs work
Content You see my signs— ____ in towns and cities. ____ in the country. ____ along streets and highways. ____ in schools and libraries. My signs tell about— ____ things to do (or not do). ____ places. ____ things people like or want.	____ 4 = Wow! ____ 3 = Strong ____ 2 = Some strengths ____ 1 = Needs work
Style ____ Each sign looks real. ____ I used different types of letters. ____ I used pictures with my signs.	____ 4 = Wow! ____ 3 = Strong ____ 2 = Some strengths ____ 1 = Needs work
Grammar and mechanics ____ I spelled words correctly. ____ I used commands correctly. ____ I capitalized the names of places.	____ 4 = Wow! ____ 3 = Strong ____ 2 = Some strengths ____ 1 = Needs work

ChecBric for Personal Web Page

Focus	Overall rating
Organization _____ My Web page gives information in groups (me, my friends, my family, etc.). _____ I used sentences to give information.	_____ 4 = Wow! _____ 3 = Strong _____ 2 = Some strengths _____ 1 = Needs work
Content The Web page tells others about... _____ me. _____ my family and friends. _____ my school. _____ my favorite things.	_____ 4 = Wow! _____ 3 = Strong _____ 2 = Some strengths _____ 1 = Needs work
Style _____ My Web page has a welcome and a logo. _____ My Web page includes photos or art that tell about me.	_____ 4 = Wow! _____ 3 = Strong _____ 2 = Some strengths _____ 1 = Needs work
Grammar and mechanics _____ I used complete sentences. _____ I made sure that *be* verbs agree with their subjects. _____ I capitalized all proper nouns.	_____ 4 = Wow! _____ 3 = Strong _____ 2 = Some strengths _____ 1 = Needs work

ChecBric for Map

Focus	Overall rating
Organization _____ My map has a title. _____ My map uses symbols and has a legend. _____ I labeled landmarks and routes. _____ My map has a one-sentence caption.	_____ 4 = Wow! _____ 3 = Strong _____ 2 = Some strengths _____ 1 = Needs work
Content _____ I drew my map to scale. _____ I put landmarks in the right location. _____ I used the correct names of landmarks and routes. _____ The map is easy to read and use.	_____ 4 = Wow! _____ 3 = Strong _____ 2 = Some strengths _____ 1 = Needs work
Style _____ I drew my map neatly. _____ I printed landmarks and routes clearly. _____ I used color in my map.	_____ 4 = Wow! _____ 3 = Strong _____ 2 = Some strengths _____ 1 = Needs work
Grammar and mechanics _____ I used a complete sentence for my caption. _____ I used a capital letter for each noun in the title. _____ All names begin with capitals.	_____ 4 = Wow! _____ 3 = Strong _____ 2 = Some strengths _____ 1 = Needs work

ChecBric for Field Guide

Focus	Overall rating
Organization ____ My title names the animal. ____ My page gives information about the animal. ____ My page has a map.	____ 4 = Wow! ____ 3 = Strong ____ 2 = Some strengths ____ 1 = Needs work
Content The information tells... ____ where the animal lives. ____ the animal's size. ____ the animal's weight. ____ what the animal eats. ____ My page also tells one amazing fact about the animal.	____ 4 = Wow! ____ 3 = Strong ____ 2 = Some strengths ____ 1 = Needs work
Style ____ My writing is easy to understand. ____ I used at least one adjective. ____ I included a picture of the animal.	____ 4 = Wow! ____ 3 = Strong ____ 2 = Some strengths ____ 1 = Needs work
Grammar and mechanics ____ I used complete sentences. ____ I made sure that all verbs agree with their subjects. ____ I used a capital letter to begin each sentence and a period to end each one.	____ 4 = Wow! ____ 3 = Strong ____ 2 = Some strengths ____ 1 = Needs work

ChecBric for How-to Instructions: Recipe

Focus	Overall rating
Organization ____ I gave my recipe a name. ____ I wrote a short introduction for my recipe. ____ I listed the utensils you will need. ____ I listed the ingredients you will need. ____ I put the steps in time order.	____ 4 = Wow! ____ 3 = Strong ____ 2 = Some strengths ____ 1 = Needs work
Content ____ I explained how much or how many of each ingredient you need. ____ Each step is accurate. ____ My recipe is "as easy as 1-2-3" to follow.	____ 4 = Wow! ____ 3 = Strong ____ 2 = Some strengths ____ 1 = Needs work
Style ____ I gave my recipe an interesting name. ____ Each sentence is short and simple.	____ 4 = Wow! ____ 3 = Strong ____ 2 = Some strengths ____ 1 = Needs work
Grammar and mechanics ____ Each instruction is complete. ____ I used the right prepositions.	____ 4 = Wow! ____ 3 = Strong ____ 2 = Some strengths ____ 1 = Needs work

ChecBric for Report: Survey

Focus	Overall rating
Organization _____ I gave my report a title. _____ My report has an introduction that asks my survey question. _____ I listed the result answers in order from the largest to the smallest number of people. _____ I named my source at the end of the survey.	_____ 4 = Wow! _____ 3 = Strong _____ 2 = Some strengths _____ 1 = Needs work
Content _____ I asked an interesting question. _____ I explained who and how many people I asked. _____ I gave accurate numbers or percentages. _____ My source is accurate.	_____ 4 = Wow! _____ 3 = Strong _____ 2 = Some strengths _____ 1 = Needs work
Style _____ My survey has an introduction. _____ I pose an interesting question that hooks the reader.	_____ 4 = Wow! _____ 3 = Strong _____ 2 = Some strengths _____ 1 = Needs work
Grammar and mechanics _____ I used complete sentences in my introduction. _____ I numbered the results in my list.	_____ 4 = Wow! _____ 3 = Strong _____ 2 = Some strengths _____ 1 = Needs work

ChecBric for Personal Memory

Focus	Overall rating
Organization ____ I wrote my memory in the first person, using "I." ____ I described events the way they happened.	____ 4 = Wow! ____ 3 = Strong ____ 2 = Some strengths ____ 1 = Needs work
Content ____ My memory describes the event or experience that is important to me. ____ I told how I felt about the event. ____ I explained why I remember the experience.	____ 4 = Wow! ____ 3 = Strong ____ 2 = Some strengths ____ 1 = Needs work
Style ____ I wrote like I was talking to the reader. ____ I used adjectives that describe my feelings.	____ 4 = Wow! ____ 3 = Strong ____ 2 = Some strengths ____ 1 = Needs work
Grammar and mechanics ____ I used complete sentences. ____ I used the right forms of past tense verbs. ____ I used a capital letter for the pronoun *I*.	____ 4 = Wow! ____ 3 = Strong ____ 2 = Some strengths ____ 1 = Needs work

ChecBric for Short Report: Our World

Focus	Overall rating
Organization ____ My title names the place. ____ My paragraph has a topic sentence. ____ I gave at least one fact to support my topic sentence.	____ 4 = Wow! ____ 3 = Strong ____ 2 = Some strengths ____ 1 = Needs work
Content ____ I told about a place that is special, or one of a kind. ____ I gave interesting facts. ____ I included a picture of the place and a map.	____ 4 = Wow! ____ 3 = Strong ____ 2 = Some strengths ____ 1 = Needs work
Style ____ My writing is easy to understand. ____ I put two sentences together into one to make my writing "flow" for the reader.	____ 4 = Wow! ____ 3 = Strong ____ 2 = Some strengths ____ 1 = Needs work
Grammar and mechanics ____ I used complete sentences. ____ I used the correct comparative and superlative adjectives. ____ I used a capital letter for the names of places and buildings.	____ 4 = Wow! ____ 3 = Strong ____ 2 = Some strengths ____ 1 = Needs work

ChecBric for Opinion Column

Focus	Overall rating
Organization _____ My title is the same as the question I asked. _____ I wrote "yes" answers first, then "no" answers. _____ I named each person who answered my question.	_____ 4 = Wow! _____ 3 = Strong _____ 2 = Some strengths _____ 1 = Needs work
Content _____ I asked an interesting question. _____ I chose the most interesting answers to report.	_____ 4 = Wow! _____ 3 = Strong _____ 2 = Some strengths _____ 1 = Needs work
Style _____ I used people's real words. _____ Each quote is accurate.	_____ 4 = Wow! _____ 3 = Strong _____ 2 = Some strengths _____ 1 = Needs work
Grammar and mechanics _____ I used the right word order for my question. _____ I used complete sentences for each answer. _____ I put quotation marks around each person's words.	_____ 4 = Wow! _____ 3 = Strong _____ 2 = Some strengths _____ 1 = Needs work

Glossary

UNIT 1

athletic—good at sports
awesome—really, really great
best—better than anyone or anything else
brat—a bad, difficult child
friend—someone you like and who likes you
hip-hop—a type of music lots of kids like
Hotmail—an Internet e-mail service

innocent—sweet or nice
loveable (*also* lovable)—easy for other people to love
popular—having a lot of friends
sleep in—to get up later than you usually do
special—different from most other people or things
sports—games people or teams play against each other
wow—what you say when something surprises you

UNIT 2

area—a part of a building, park, office, etc., for doing something
avalanche—snow, ice, and rocks that fall off a mountain side
crossing—a place where you can go from one side of the street to the other
danger—a harmful situation
deposit—to put something into something else
detour—a different way of going from one place to another

diner—a restaurant with simple food and low prices
fly rod caster—someone who fishes with a special type of fishing pole
frisbee heaver—someone who throws a Frisbee
recycle—to use things again that people throw away
special treat—something good to eat
spray can sprayer—someone who uses a spray can to paint on a wall

UNIT 3

attend—to go to class or school regularly
auto wholesaler—someone who sells cars
brand—the name of the company that makes something
chorus—a group of people who sing together
enjoy—to like doing something
exercising—doing activities that make you strong and healthy
favorite—liked better than anything else
future—any time after right now
future plans—what you want to do when you are older
goal—something you hope to do one day
graduate— to finish high school, college, or some other educational program
heights—high places

hobby—an activity you do for fun, usually by yourself
hometown—the place you come from
honor roll—a list recognizing students who get all A's and B's
nickname—a name your friends call you
personal living—a class that teaches you skills for everyday life
role model—a person you want to be like
size—how big or small something is
successful—good at what you do
Super Bowl—the championship football game played every year in January
Vikings—Minnesota's football team
welcome—a friendly greeting

UNIT 4

curve—to move like part of a circle
direction—the way someone or something is facing, moving, or located in relation to you
Earth—the planet we live on
enter—to go in
equal—to be the same as
flat—without any high or low areas
foot—a unit for measuring length (= 12 inches or 30.5 centimeters)

imaginary—not real
inch—a unit for measuring short lengths (= 1/12 of a foot or 2.54 centimeters)
lamplight—the light from a lamp
mile—a U.S./English unit used to measure long distances (= 5,280 feet or 1.6 kilometers)
round—shaped like a ball or the letter "o"
travel—to go places
wrap around—to go all the way around

UNIT 5

address—the street name and number where someone lives or works
blazing—very hot
breed—a type of animal
caiman—a type of crocodile
clover—a grasslike plant with three round leaves
cud—food already eaten once, then brought back into the mouth
dandelion—a plant with tiny yellow flowers
domestic—used to describe an animal that lives with people or works on a farm
gigantic—very large
grain—crops like corn, wheat, or rice
greater than—more than
hare—a wild rabbit
herb—a plant used for flavor in cooking
hug—to use arms or legs to squeeze

mate—the partner of an animal
nectar—sweet liquid in flowers
pasture—grassland where cattle feed
pop—to break
poultry—birds like chickens and turkeys
pound—a unit used to measure weight (= 16 ounces or 454 grams)
savannah—grassland
size—how big or how small something is
submerged—under water
sunburned—used to describe skin that is burned by the sun
swallow—to make food go down your throat
swamplands—land that is covered with water
tapir—an animal with a heavy body and short legs
weight—how heavy or how light something is
wild boar—a type of wild pig
yawn—to open your mouth wide when you are sleepy

UNIT 6

add—to put something else in with other things
adventurous—willing to try new and different things
baking pan—a metal pan used to cook or bake food in the oven
baloney—something silly or not true
Big Apple—a nickname for New York City
bread knife—a tool you use to slice bread
can opener—a tool you use to open cans
chicken—afraid
crashing—making a sudden loud noise
crumb—a very small piece of bread or cake
difficulty—how easy or hard it is to do something
eat your words—to admit being wrong
feather—one of the light, soft things that cover a bird
glass measuring cup—a cup used to measure large amounts of ingredients
knife—a sharp tool used to cut food into small pieces
measuring cup—a cup used to measure ingredients
measuring spoons—tools used to measure small amounts
medium—in between; moderate
melted—very hot, soft and gooey
microwave oven—a machine used to heat food very quickly
mixing bowl—a bowl you use to mix ingredients
nostalgic—making you remember happy past times
optional—possible, but not necessary
oven—a machine used to bake or broil food

oven mitt—something you wear on your hand when you take a hot pan out of the oven
oz.—ounce
piece of cake—very easy
pizza cutter—a tool you use to cut pizzas
plate—a flat dish used to serve food on
preheat—to heat an oven to a certain temperature before putting food in it
saucepan—a small, deep metal pan used to cook food on the stove
seasoned—having flavor from herbs, spices, or salt
serving—the amount of a food that one person eats
set—to become solid
shape—to form something with your hands
spatula—a tool used to lift, turn, or flip pieces of food
spill the beans—to tell a secret
spray—to put a liquid onto something using a pressurized can
sprinkle—to scatter tiny pieces of something on something else
swirling—going around and around
tbsp.—tablespoon
tsp.—teaspoon
type—a kind
wedge—a piece of something, shaped like a triangle
whisk—a tool used to beat or whip liquids
wooden spoon—a spoon used to stir or mix food together

UNIT 7

according to—said or written by someone
assignment—a piece of schoolwork
beat the heat—to stay cool when the weather is hot
beverage—something to drink
broken—cracked in pieces

close second—a person or thing that is almost in first place
core—the center of something, like an apple
crumpled—crushed into a ball
number one—the best or most important person or thing
overdue—late being returned to the library

percent—the amount in every hundred
pick—the best thing out of a group
prefer—to like something better than something else
recess—free time during the school day
reed—a thin piece of wood attached to the mouthpiece of an instrument to help it make a sound
researcher—someone who studies a subject
rotten—going bad or decaying

series—a set of things, like books, that come one after another
source—a person or book you get information from
sugary—having a lot of sugar in it
survey—a set of question you ask other people to find out what they like or think
temperature—how hot or cold something is

UNIT 8

afraid of—frightened by something
all-star—involving only the top athletes
grave—the place where a dead body is buried
league—a group of sports teams that play against each other
legend—someone who is famous for being very good at something
ligament—one of the "bands" that hold your bones together
lose—to come in last in a game or contest
offensive guard—the person in a football game who plays guard when his or her team has the ball

sled—to ride a vehicle that slides over snow
softball—a game like baseball except that a larger, softer ball is used
surprise—a feeling you have when something happens that you don't expect
tore—the past tense of the verb *tear*, which means to rip or split apart
touchdown—the action of moving the football into the other team's end zone to score points
uniform—clothing worn by team members
win—to be first in a game or contest

UNIT 9

bay—an area of water with land around most of it (smaller than a gulf)
canyon—a deep valley with very steep sides
considered—thought to be true by most people
continental—relating to a continent
continent—one of the seven great areas of land: Africa, Antarctica, Asia, Australia, Europe, North America, and South America
feet—the plural of *foot*, a unit for measuring length (1 foot = 12 inches or 30.5 centimeters)
gulf—an area of ocean with land around most of it (larger than a bay)

mightier—stronger; bigger
mile—a unit for measuring long distances (= 5,280 feet or 1.6 kilometers)
peak—the top of a very tall mountain
peninsula—land with water on three sides
plain—a large area of very flat land
prairie—a large area of flat land with tall grasses and few trees
sea level—the height of the water in the oceans
summit—the top of a mountain
valley—a low place between two mountains

UNIT 10

action—exciting things that happen
all over—everywhere you look
allowed—having permission to do something
bat—a long wooden stick used for hitting a baseball
blue—sad
challenge—something new or difficult that requires skill
chop—a piece of meat
comfortable—at ease or relaxed
crack—a loud noise that sounds like something breaking
different—not like something or someone else
dunk—to push a basketball through the hoop at close range
embarrassed—feeling shy or ashamed in front of other people
fast-paced—having lots of action
feast—a large meal, often for many people
home run—a long hit in baseball in which the hitter is able to run around all the bases and score a point

lobster—an ocean shellfish with large claws
on the ball—able to think quickly
out of style—not in fashion or popular any more
outdoor experiences—activities like camping and fishing
pressure—a feeling that you have too much work and other things to do
skill—the ability to do something very well
still—continuing until now or until a particular time
stress—worries that keep you from relaxing
sunny—happy
thankless—unpleasant and without thankful feelings
till—until
viewpoint—what someone believes or thinks
year-round school—schools that are open all year. Students have many short vacations rather than a long summer vacation.

Common Irregular Verbs

Simple Form	Past Form	Past Participle	Simple Form	Past Form	Past Participle
be	was/were	been	lay (= put)	laid	laid
beat	beat	beaten	lead	led	led
become	became	become	leave	left	left
begin	began	begun	let	let	let
bend	bent	bent	lie (= lie down)	lay	lain
bite	bit	bitten	lose	lost	lost
break	broke	broken	make	made	made
bring	brought	brought	mean	meant	meant
build	built	built	meet	met	met
buy	bought	bought	pay	paid	paid
catch	caught	caught	put	put	put
choose	chose	chosen	quit	quit	quit
come	came	come	read	read	read
cost	cost	cost	ride	rode	ridden
cut	cut	cut	ring	rang	rung
do	did	done	rise	rose	risen
draw	drew	drawn	run	ran	run
drink	drank	drunk	say	said	said
eat	ate	eaten	see	saw	seen
fall	fell	fallen	sell	sold	sold
feed	fed	fed	send	sent	sent
feel	felt	felt	set	set	set
fight	fought	fought	show	showed	shown
find	found	found	shut	shut	shut
fly	flew	flown	sing	sang	sung
forget	forgot	forgotten	sit	sat	sat
forgive	forgave	forgiven	sleep	slept	slept
get	got	gotten	speak	spoke	spoken
give	gave	given	spend	spent	spent
go	went	gone	stand	stood	stood
grow	grew	grown	swim	swam	swum
have	had	had	take	took	taken
hear	heard	heard	teach	taught	taught
hide	hid	hidden	tear	tore	torn
hit	hit	hit	tell	told	told
hold	held	held	think	thought	thought
hurt	hurt	hurt	throw	threw	thrown
keep	kept	kept	understand	understood	understood
know	knew	known	wake	woke	woken

Listening Script

UNIT 1

A. 1. Tuning In. (page 4)

1. I like many things. I like to eat. I like pizza. What about you?
2. I like burritos. What about you?
3. I like ice cream. What about you?
4. I like French fries. What about you?
5. I also like sports. I like baseball. What about you?
6. I like soccer. What about you?
7. I like football. What about you?
8. And I *love* music! I like hip-hop. What about you?
9. I like country music. What about you?
10. I like many things. Do *you*?

UNIT 2

A. 1. Tuning In. (page 22)

Conversation one
Girl: Excuse me, I'm looking for Ms. Flores
Boy: Her office is at the end of the hall. There's a sign on her door. It says, "PRINCIPAL'S OFFICE."

Conversation two
Boy: How far is it? I'm tired!
Girl: There's a sign over there. It says "LOS ANGELES, 65 MILES."

Conversation three
Woman: I need to buy just one more thing.
Man: I'll find a place to sit and wait for you.
Woman: Where will I meet you?

Man: Near the sign that says "INFORMATION," right in front of the Toy Department.

Conversation four
Woman: We need milk.
Girl: Where do I find it?
Woman: See the sign that says "DAIRY"? It's over there.

Conversation five
Girl: Hurry up, Carlos! We can still cross...!
Boy: We'd better wait. That sign says "DON'T WALK."

UNIT 3

A. 1. Tuning In. (page 40)

Lori: What are you doing? Playing on the computer?
Maria: I'm making my own Web page. You can help me. What kind of things do I put on my Web page?
Lori: Hmm. Tell me about you ... *and* about your family, too.
Maria: Well...I have one sister and two brothers.
Lori: What do you like to do for fun?
Maria: I like to go to the mall... and watch TV.
Lori: What TV shows do you like a lot?

Maria: The Simpsons! I *love* The Simpsons.
Lori: What about food? What do you like?
Maria: Pizza.
Lori: What kind of music do you like?
Maria: Hip-hop.
Lori: What are you good at? What subject do you like best?
Maria: I like math.
Lori: This is an interesting Web page!

A. 1. Tuning In. (page 58)

Diego: What street are we on?

Juan: We're on Palisade Avenue. Keep going on Palisade. When we get to New School Street, turn.

Diego: Which way?

Juan: Uh ...turn right. And then it looks like we go two more blocks ... then turn left.

Diego: On to what street?

Juan: Maple. Then we turn right again, on to Linden. The address is... *OH, NO*! I forgot to write down the address!

A. 1. Tuning In. (page 76)

Eduardo: My name is Eduardo Valdez.

Brian: And my name is Brian Lee. We both travel around the world to find amazing, or interesting, animals.

Eduardo: Last year, Brian and I were in South America. We were looking for giant snakes. We study reptiles—animals like snakes, lizards, and alligators.

Brian: We were walking in a swamp—a place with a lot of water.

Eduardo: There was a dead tree in front of me, lying on the ground. And so, I stepped on it. Suddenly, it moved! It wasn't a tree at all!

Brian: It was a HUGE snake! It was about 20 feet long and as thick as my leg. I was scared! This snake was so big he could eat us both!

Eduardo: The snake twisted around my body, then my neck. Snakes like that kill you! They don't kill you with poison. They crush you to death!

Brian: That's right! Some snakes kill you by biting you. And some snakes kill you by crushing, or squeezing, you to death.

Eduardo: Brian thought fast. He pulled the snake loose.

Brian: Yes, I pulled the snake loose! Then it disappeared into the water.

Eduardo: Brian saved my life! I was really scared!

Brian: So was I! I was really scared, too!

D. 1. Word Detective (page 80)

1. A thread snake is very tiny.
2. An anaconda is huge.
3. A king snake is a very large snake.
4. A brown snake weighs less than a pound.
5. An anaconda weighs up to 100 pounds.
6. A boa constrictor can grow to over 8 feet long.
7. A brown snake is no longer than a foot.
8. A thread snake weighs only two or three ounces.

A. 1. Tuning In (page 94)

Boy: Hey, Mom, let's have burritos for dinner.

Mother: OK. I'll show you how to make them. First, let's take out the ingredients. We'll need tortillas, shredded chicken, beans, and rice.

Boy: What's "shredded" chicken?

Mother: That means it's torn in tiny pieces.

Boy: What about cheese?

Mother: Right! We need cheese. OK, let's take out the large skillet.

Boy: Here it is.

Mother: Turn on the stove. We need to warm the tortillas in the skillet first, to make them soft. Here ... you can heat the first one.

Boy: Here's the first tortilla. It's really hot.

Mother: OK, now watch me. First you add the rice. Then you add the beans. After that you add the chicken...and you sprinkle the cheese on top of the chicken.... Next you wrap the tortilla around the filling.

Then you roll the burrito up really tight. Put it in the microwave oven for a few seconds to make it hot.

Boy: Yummmmm.... This is really good!
Mother: Now you know how to make a burrito.

UNIT 7

A. 1. Tuning In. (page 112)

Interviewer: Do you all like pizza?
All: Yes!
Boy #1: It's my favorite food!
Girl: I love pizza!
Boy #2: Pizza's my favorite, too!
Interviewer: What's your favorite topping—besides cheese?

Boy #2: Pepperoni. I always order pepperoni.
Boy #1: I like sausage.
Girl: My favorite topping is ham and pineapple.
Boy #1 and Boy #2: *Pineapple!*
Interviewer: What about anchovies? Does anybody like anchovies?
All: Eeeewww! Yuck!

UNIT 8

A. 1. Tuning In. (page 130)

Bernie Davis: I remember a Little League game when I was eight. I had no idea how to play baseball. I ended up hitting the ball for the winning base hit. But afterward, I had to ask the coach who won the game!

UNIT 9

A. 1. Tuning In. (page 148)

1. Girl: A mountain is higher than a hill.
2. Boy: A stream is wider than a river.
3. Girl: A pool is bigger than a lake.

4. Boy: An ocean is deeper than a lake.
5. Girl: A river is longer than a stream.

UNIT 10

A. 1 Tuning In. (page 166)

Juan: Do you want to watch TV?
Lori: You watch too much TV. It isn't good for you to watch TV.
Juan: What are you talking about? TV is good for you.
Lori: No, it isn't. If you watch TV, you don't have time for homework.

Juan: But you learn a lot from TV.
Lori: You learn more from reading books.
Juan: TV is interesting.
Lori: TV is *silly*. It's a waste of time. Kids who watch a lot of TV don't do well in school.
Juan: But I get A's and B's!
Lori: If you don't watch TV, you'll get all A's.

H. 1.5. Writer's Workshop—Getting It Out—Activity 5. (page 177)

Lori: Should kids have to take PE?
1. Boy #1: Yes! Kids need exercise.
2. Girl #1: No! Most kids hate taking showers at school.

3. Boy #2: No! You don't learn anything in PE!
4. Girl #2: Yes! PE teaches you teamwork.
5. Boy #3: No! Other classes are more important.
6. Girl #3: Yes! PE makes you feel better.

Index

Text and Audio Credits

Photo Credits